Are we
there
yet?

Other books from *The Sun*:

The Ultimate Guide to Baltimore Schools

Miss Prudence Pennypack's Perfectly Proper,
    by Karen E. Rupprecht

A Century In The Sun: Photographs of Maryland

A Century In The Sun: Front Pages of the Twentieth Century

A Century In The Sun: Postcards of Maryland's Past

Dining in Baltimore: Food And Drink In And Around Charm City

Hometown Boy: The Hoodle Patrol and Other Curiosities of Baltimore, by Rafael Alvarez

The Wild Side of Maryland, An Outdoor Guide, 2nd Edition

The Great Game of Maryland Politics, by Barry Rascovar

Gaining A Yard: The Building of Baltimore's Football Stadium, by Jon Morgan and Doug Kapustin

Raising Kids & Tomatoes, by Rob Kasper

Motherhood Is A Contact Sport, by Susan Reimer

The 1996-1997 Maryland Business Almanac

Cal Touches Home

This *Baltimore Sun* book was published by SunSource, the information service of *The Sun*. To order any of the above titles, or for information on research, reprints and information from the paper's archives, please call 410.332.6800.

Are we there yet?

Recollections of life's many journeys

A collection of columns from 1974 – 1999

Elise T. Chisolm

THE BALTIMORE SUN

Published by
 The Baltimore Sun
A Times Mirror company
501 N. Calvert Street
Baltimore, MD 21278

Edited by Melinda Greenberg
Layout and design by Jennifer Halbert
Copy edited by Ray Frager

Cover photo by Photo Disc
Photo of Ms. Chisolm by Jim Burger

ISBN — 1-893116-10-7
Library of Congress in ppublication data applied for.

Are we there yet? Recollections of life's many journeys : a publication of The Baltimore Sun Company — 1999 — Baltimore, MD: Baltimore Sun Co.: 1999

In memory of Guy Chisolm

Contents:

Foreword : Seize the Day

Life is a little like a long train ride, isn't it? And there are many stations. Many years ago, author and minister Robert J. Hastings wrote a cogent essay that likened life to "the train ride and the stations." I recall this piece, called "The Station," which Ann Landers reprinted in 1997.

He wrote: "Tucked away in our subconscious is an idyllic vision. We see ourselves on a long trip that spans the continent... but sooner or later we must realize there is no station, no one place to arrive; once and for all. The true joy of life is the trip."

Lastly, he added, "So, stop pacing the aisles and counting the miles. Instead, climb more mountains, eat more ice cream, go barefoot more often, swim more rivers, watch more sunsets, laugh more, cry less."

In other words, *carpe diem*, seize the day, and once I did. I have never regretted it.

It was April of 1943, a war raged, and I made the decision to take a train across the country from Philadelphia to Tacoma, Wash., and marry a Naval officer. Guy was a Texan I met on a blind date, and with whom I had fallen madly in love three months prior to our small wedding in Tacoma. Fifty-four years of a good marriage followed. That was my biggest station and a risky one. One that changed forever an 18-year-old girl's life. The trip to the West Coast was a long train ride with troops on every car. I almost changed my mind in Chicago. I got off the train and called my mother and cried, "I think I don't want to do this. ... I'm scared." She told me I couldn't disappoint him; she loved him, too. Just to hear her strong voice was all I needed to go on and get back on that train. Hastings would have approved of the risk.

My husband and I had a small wedding in Tacoma in a friend's house. Then I traveled the West Coast with two other Navy wives, chasing the ship from port to port until it left in much pomp and ceremony to fight in the Pacific theater. His ship was hit twice and limped in to Okinawa. And soon, after that terrible time, it was VJ day and he came home. A triumphant time for those who survived. That's when I learned independence and when I grew up. I became happily married and was in love with the man I married and the West Coast, too. I was far from home but never homesick.

I grew up in Bryn Mawr, Pa., and I wanted to be a famous tennis player. But when I was 12, while a student at the Baldwin School in Bryn Mawr, an English teacher, who was elderly and sage, told me I must always write. I had read aloud a story I had written about the death of a rose in the garden. The class cried. So I decided to be a writer first and then a tennis player.

At that awkward age, I had become withdrawn and shy, and I wrote what I felt, a poem, a story, a letter, anything that would make people laugh or cry and leave me talking to myself through the written word, overcoming my shyness.

I thought I was on my way to Bryn Mawr College, but life changed. My mother divorced my father when I was 15. My siblings and I supported this, and we moved happily into an apartment. My father was a figure head father. I never really got to know him. Mother was a dynamic woman, ahead of her time. An early feminist, she became a lecturer later in life and was always in demand. A specialist in women of the Bible and Edgar Allan Poe, she held one of two part-time jobs even after she was 60. Then she came to live with us in Texas where we had settled after the war.

By the time my husband was in business in Texas, we had four children. I attended West Texas State University at night between the births of the children. I had a wonderful teacher, Texas author-professor Lou Grace Erdman (everyone in Texas then had a double name), a novelist and encourager of young writers. She told me I had to write. So I did, again. From then on, I knew I would write for a living and for my soul. I went to work for the *Amarillo Globe News* with a weekly column in the 1950s.

I worked for three other newspapers — *The Amarillo Citizen*, the *Anne Arundel Star* and then 26 years at the Baltimore *Evening Sun*. I have been published in four national magazines, and my column in the *Evening Sun* was carried over the *Los Angeles Times-Washington Post* News Service to many cities and Canada.

But my life has always centered around my four children, now grown, ranging from 41 to 55. Being a mother has been one of the fullest — and hardest — jobs I've ever had. My children are very different from one another, which puzzles me, some liberal, some conservative, some blond, some dark-haired. Therefore, I don't get them mixed up. We have never had their DNA tested. Oh, they are good people. No one has been in jail, yet. But their ratings could change tomorrow.

Once, when we were moving, I threw out some Barbie doll stuff, a headless Ken doll, and I was put on report for years by the two girls. And things were sour when I had to tell them at 10 there was no more tooth fairy.

My experiences interviewing people for the Baltimore *Evening Sun* were the zaniest and most rewarding of my career. From going in the wrong door of the White House, where President Lyndon Johnson ushered me in — I was scheduled to go upstairs for an appointment with Lady Bird's social secretary — to lying down on a grassy knoll at the Merriweather Post Pavilion with Burt Bacharach for an interview so he could sunbathe to talking to Victor Borge at Oregon Ridge State Park while he slipped off the park bench to talking to a clown at the circus while sitting on a crate containing alligators. Or just talking with Vincent Price: "How could any man not believe in something or someone larger than himself, bigger than life…" as he looked at me with those Dracula eyes.

And then Carroll O'Connor told me in 1974 he was tired of playing archbigot Archie Bunker. After an interview with Mickey Rooney, he asked me to play golf with him. I recall he was married at the time to his sixth wife. But he was too young for me and I was too tall for him.

Celebrities are easy to interview, because they do all the talking.

My career was a nice blend of work and play. I can't talk about my time at the *Evening Sun* without mentioning the 10 years of chronic back pain I struggled with. Three operations in the 1970s failed to help and I coped with a body cast, traction, other painful procedures, trips to healers and out-of-town doctors for their opinions. My chronic pain hurt my family and interfered with my writing and my career. (I am presently writing a book about how I overcame my chronic back pain.) And then I found a miracle — an alternative procedure called Trigger Point Therapy — that finally made me well. But I learned one thing in those long years; you can survive pain. It taught me enduring patience, empathy for others and infinite hope and faith. At any time, the loss of a sense of humor is the ultimate loss, second only to the loss of your health and the one you love.

A widow now, I realize what I miss most of all is the support of the man I loved so long. I really believe that my mother and my husband, whose faith was strong, have met in heaven and formed a bond to be absolutely sure I do the right thing and become a person who makes a difference. A writer is what they would want me to be, a writer forever, as long as my forever lasts.

Elise Chisolm
Baltimore, MD
Sept. 3, 1999

Chapter 1

The
*War
Bride:*
Battles on the Home Front

Room Service for Breakfast — Ah, Those Good Old Days

Have you called for room service lately?

Well, my husband and I spent the night in a motel outside of New York City recently. Here's what happened.

The next morning, he announced, "Let's call room service, and have breakfast in bed."

"Honey, I don't think they do that anymore. Besides, they didn't give us any bath towels, so I hardly think they'd give us breakfast in bed. But you can call and try," I answered.

"No, you call. A woman's voice is more convincing nowadays."

"Wow, I can remember before World War II when I spent a night in a New York hotel. They left a rose on my pillow and they turned down my bed," I commented nostalgically.

"That must have been before I met you."

"It was." (Sigh.)

"We'll call, anyway," he said.

"Wait, when he comes with the tray, I don't have a bathrobe, just this white see-through nightie. Where will I go?"

"Get under the covers," he suggested.

"What will you do? You don't have any pajamas." (Since Navy days he's slept in his skivvies.)

"Well, we'll both get under the covers."

"That's ridiculous at our age," I told him.

"Look, I know, remember on our honeymoon at the St. Regis we just asked them to leave the breakfast outside the door?" (Our honeymoon was in Victoria, British Columbia, but never mind).

"Are you kidding? Someone would steal it before we could run and get it," I said.

"OK, look, we'll both get dressed to receive the trays, then get undressed to eat the breakfast," he announced triumphantly.

"How absurd. And weird. Why order breakfast in bed then?"

"OK, I've got it, I'll stay under the covers, then you just wrap the bed-spread around you and go to the door when they come. Let's decide what we want for breakfast."

We argued and debated for a half-hour over whether we wanted scrambled or fried eggs, sausage or bacon.

"All right," I said, "I've got it written down, I'll call."

Now hear this: "Room service? I'd like, first, some bath towels, and then I'd like to order two breakfasts."

"Oh, I'm so sorry," said room service, "but we don't have room service in the summer. We do have a nice coffee shop. And we can't get you the bath towels until 11 a.m. which is our checkout time."

I put the phone down. Well, after all, it wasn't the St. Regis. It was 1974.

Directions by Moon: But That's the Sun

It may be a little thing in your life, and I hope it is, but it's a big thing in mine. The road map.

It's my nemesis. In all the years of our marriage, we've argued more over road maps and directions than money and in-laws.

I never believe in going anywhere without one, or two or three or a dozen.

My husband says they aren't correct and that he not only doesn't need them but also that they are outdated, and really just concentrate on the 13 colonies.

Once he told me St. Louis had been moved on the map he was using. He also doesn't believe in asking directions.

The other night, coming back from Philadelphia a new way, we got lost. I got out the road map.

"Please don't turn on the light in the car; it distracts the driver. We're not lost," he declared.

"Well, how come we haven't seen a person, a house, a light or a street sign for an hour. I'll light the cigarette lighter and see if I can read by that."

Now, I'm not very dexterous with road maps. Usually, I have to turn the map upside down if we're going south. Then I can't fold the map back to its original creases. This infuriates me.

He can fold a map. But I would never give him the satisfaction of asking.

Folding a road map in a car is like folding a contour sheet in a tent, or changing a baby for the first time — you think you know how to do it, but things just don't look right.

So on car trips when I have to fold maps, I also sit on them. Once I pressed a road map all the way from Tulsa to Los Angeles — so well that no one knew it wasn't brand new.

"If you'll pull over to the side of the road, I can tell you exactly where we are," I pleaded. "I've even found Pennsylvania on the map in the dark."

"No, we'll lose time if I stop. This road will go somewhere and then it will lead us back to the main highway. Anyway, it's nice going on a new road for a change."

"Oh, wait, there's a road sign. Route 341," he went on.

I checked the map by the cigarette lighter and my sore eyes lit up. "There's no Route 341. We're lost — 341 is the population of the town you just went through."

"We couldn't be lost, Pennsylvania isn't that big," he insisted. "Throw the map out. As long as we're heading south and the moon is over my right shoulder, we're OK."

He drove another 80 miles or so. Then he gloated. "I just saw a sign saying Richmond, Va. — and don't look that up; I know where that city is."

"But we're only going to Baltimore," I reminded him.

"Don't worry. The moon is still over my right shoulder," he replied, yawning.

"Dummy, that's the sun coming up."

How to Report Fender-Bender to Hubby When You Were Driver

How to tell your husband about your car wreck? Well, here are some hints.

When you are first married, say the first 10 years, you call him from a phone booth or a police station and cry. And he comes running to get you, hugs you, kisses you and usually says, "Darling, as long as you aren't hurt, we don't care about that little, old totaled car."

Later, say the second 10 years, you call after you've calmed down. Tell him like this: "I've had a minor accident, dear, nothing serious. I backed out of the garage, but the door was closed. It's nothing to worry about, because I'm OK."

Make it seem like you're reporting your second pregnancy — almost exciting, but with some reservation.

After you've been married, say, 30 years, you don't call him if you can help it. You call the insurance agent. In fact, if you can get home before he does, hide the car in the garage, if it's drivable.

Get everything up with the insurance companies, and feel your own neck and back to see if you have whiplash. Take your own pulse and be a big girl. Don't cry on the phone, if you have to call your husband.

Here's how I did it last week. I had to tell him about the car wreck before he came home because we don't have a garage. I called him.

"Hi, dear," I said. "Are you having a nice day?"

"Yeah, are you?" he asked.

"Oh, yes, it's lovely and sunny here. Does everyone like the new necktie and shirt I gave you?"

"Yes. How's Hattie's cold?" (Hattie's the dog.)

"Look," I said, "I just wanted to tell you I had a funny, little, old, four-car collision on the way home, just a little fender-bender."

"What did you say? The connection is bad. Speak up."

"A man just bumped into the rear of the car and I hit the girl in front of me and she hit the man in front of her and ... it was a blast, ha ha."

"How's the car?" he asked.

"Oh, it's fine, just a little dent in the back fender," I assured him. "I called the insurance agent, and he was lovely. As a matter of fact, he sounded like he'd been waiting to hear from me all day. It was sort of fun sitting in that police car with five people, and that red light blinking at the top."

Grill Grouch Hauled Over Coals

We call him "the charcoaler," or just plain "grill grouch." He gets like a demon or dragon when he starts his outdoors cooking. In fact, I think he could light the fire with sparks from his tongue when he places those first coals in the grill.

Everyone tries to get out of the way of the supercook. And you can't ask questions like, "Can I have mine rare, Dad?" or "Will you take the fat off for me?" or "Can I have just a half of one, Dad?"

The happy image of the Man of the House cooking over the fire in the summer, substituting for the Woman of the House, who has cooked at least 345 dinners all winter long, is a dream. That's wishful or dishful thinking. It's hardly worth the aggravation.

Here's a typical scene. We're even into reruns. The counter tops — in fact, the whole kitchen — is lined with the raw hamburger patties he's preparing. Like a surgeon planning a brain transplant, he has put all the utensils and ingredients out, and no one must breathe on them or look at them.

He marinates secretly. He seasons furtively. One wonders could he be poisoning all of us, and then we'll never ask another question. There's a fly crawling on the meat — no, it's a piece of parsley.

At 7:15 p.m., we are all seated at the table playing 20 questions. I find I have to suggest, "I think the coals are ready, dear, they are turning gray." (So am I, but he doesn't notice.)

At 8:15 p.m., the kids are playing tic-tac-toe on their paper napkins, so I dare to say, "Dear, I think the meat is done." (My cole slaw and bean salad are done — I picked the stuff up at the deli six hours earlier.)

But his expression is still dragonly and mean.

At 9:15 p.m., the kids just ate their paper napkins. And I contemplate a Big Mac attack.

Suddenly, his expression changes. "The charcoaler" is triumphant. He yells, "OK, I hope you all are ready." He marches in from the backyard, where by now we all thought he'd been performing some tribal fire rite.

"Don't they look just great? And smell that smell!"

However, we can't smell because we have inhaled smoky fumes for so long.

But breathes there a child so brazen who would dare to say, "This hamburger tastes like the soles of my tennis shoes" or "You ought to taste the way Jody's dad grills them?"

At this hour, not too likely.

Handling Him at Tax Time: Have Your Calculator Handy

Now that April 15 — income tax deadline — has come and gone, I can take time to tell you what I've learned about the care and handling of husbands at tax time.

Around March 1, a crisis atmosphere begins to build up at our house.

I mean, any subject I bring up seems to get a reply like, "Why did she have to have ballet lessons this year?" or "Where are all the receipts from the drug store that you hung on a hanger in your closet?"

You have to be on the alert — and have all explanations and expenditures ranging from the ballet lessons to the cat's flea collar.

He is wallowing in canceled checks and self-pity. The less you are in his way, the longer your marriage will last.

Here are a few pointers that I consider as important as your family's 1040 form:

Don't talk much about anything.

Don't tell him to file early. This just makes him put the tax task off longer.

Don't tell him about any household breakdowns, even yours, that might upset his concentration — and his calculations.

In fact, you might induce him to register at a local motel for the last few days before April 15. Establish regular visiting hours.

If you have access to the checkbook, build up a cash reserve in case he had underestimated what the tax bill will be. And if he boasts that he's going to save enough to pay for a super vacation, DON'T make the reservations until you see the bottom-line figures.

Be sweet and sexy. Point out the advantages of marriage — all those dependents, not to mention the joint tax return.

He will be near the boiling point and dizzy from figuring during the final countdown. After he hands you the tax return, send him to bed with a strong nightcap.

Then, when he's asleep, get out your calculator and check his arithmetic.

Husband Offers To Do the Grocery Shopping

Once upon a time there was a couple who had four kids and who was trying its best to budget and save.

So one day, the husband said, "Look, dear, you've been doing the grocery shopping for years. Why don't you let me do it for a while?

"I think I can show you how we can economize. I'll just bet you $50 that I can get more for our money and we'll eat better, too."

During the first year, the housewife-mother had to record that at times he followed the list, and other times he brought home things like the following: six cans of beets, because they were on sale (but no one in the house liked beets); 10 jars of sardines, because he had a hankering for them at the time (but no one in the house liked sardines); a bushel basket of wormy apples, because they were on sale, that caused the housewife-mother to have to make four apple pies and two jars of applesauce, immediately; and six boxes of an off-brand detergent because they had free plastic mugs in each one.

Once she asked him to bring home 20 pounds of sugar. He forgot that but brought home five jars of molasses.

After the second year of the housewife-mother writing notes to the grocery-store husband, like "please get us a certain brand of toothpaste, or a certain brand of furniture wax," she realized it was turning their refrigerator and cupboards into sort of a marital battleground.

How did it really work out? Well, dear readers, it ended one Saturday when the husband brought home 12 boxes of dried cereal because each box had a free rubber duck inside.

"But the kids don't play with rubber ducks anymore, remember, they are older," she reminded him, while stomping her feet on the cereal boxes.

"The inflation, all the figuring has affected you, too, as it did me. I'll take over now. And oh, yes, I need my $50 to start with."

So the couple kissed and made up and lived happily ever after and the husband went back to washing his car or playing golf on Saturday mornings.

It's Just You, Me and the Phone

For the first time in years and years of married life, we are alone. Really alone.

No children for two whole weeks. They are finally old enough to go on summer vacation by themselves. Just the cat and the dog decided to stay on with us.

How I've dreamed of this time in our lives. I had thought it would be two weeks of "golden age" honeymoon bliss.

"Just think, dear, we'll get to know each other again. ..."

In my mind, I planned:

- Just cooking for two, no big meal planning.
- Only a few dishes and not much laundry.
- Or maybe eating out at least every other night.
- We'll have people in for dinner whom the kids don't like or who don't like the kids.
- We might take in an all-night drive-in.
- We'll read together Alistair Cook's book, "America," which he just got for Father's Day.
- We'll discuss life in Australia and whether we really want to go there.
- I'll start a hobby — knitting. Everyone has urged me to have a "hand hobby," insisting that it calms nerves.
- We might even take a bicycle trip, while the kids aren't here to laugh. We might even roller skate.

Well, it's been six days now, and we have not done or said anything. We can't find anything to talk about, not even to the cat and dog. I'm cooking more, because I'm making delicacies that the kids don't like. So I have more dishes.

"Why do I have so many dishes? How could we possibly have 16 glasses in one day, with just the two of us?" I asked him.

"I'll tell you why. It's been hot and we're bored, and we're drinking more

— prune juice, daiquiris, milk shakes. And last night you wanted orange concentrate mixed with club soda before you went to bed."

"But why do I have so many clothes to wash? Are you coming home for lunch and changing your clothes, or are you dressing for dinner, like your father used to?"

"Look," he said, "let's get paper plates and paper cups and paper clothes. Let's just eat TV dinners. Stop fixing me those quiche lorraines."

"Let's face it," I commented, "we should have more kids. We are lonely, and I can't stand the no noise."

"I know," he said, brightening. "Let's go to bed earlier — say, 8:30 tonight."

"Wait, we tried that last night, remember? We woke up at 4 a.m. I think we're just too old to be left to our resources, and I wish the telephone would ring."

Chapter 2

The
Happy
Hour?

The In-The-Corner Game
Is Popular — and It's Rotten

Call it the professional in-the-corner game. It's played everywhere and it's rotten.

We went to a big cocktail party the other night, and I saw a clump of women surrounding one man. I thought, "Wow, he must be an actor, an honest politician, a racing car driver — but someone famous."

Know what he was?

A local gynecologist.

The hostess, Beth, told me the next day that whenever she has him over, women surround him. And he wasn't even good-looking.

She told me they started out asking him benign questions like "How many children do you have, doctor?" or "How many babies have you delivered this year?" and so forth.

But then they closed in on him and the questions got more personal. One woman asked, "Doctor, do you think I ought to get off the birth-control pill?" (She was 62.)

I, personally, heard one girl ask if he believed in Masters and Johnson. He said, "Yes, and I believe in the Smith Brothers, the Smothers Brothers and Sonny and Cher."

In fact, Beth says he has pleaded with her to introduce him as just plain "Bill." But she says they always find out anyway. Maybe it's the way he lights his pipe or the way he takes off his coat. Who knows?

Others get cornered. But that's awful. You'd think people would have more manners at a party, anyway. I mean, the closest I've come to seeking professional help for free was asking a plumbing contractor — who was choking on a piece of chicken liver — if he'd ever tried those liquid drain cleaners. He didn't laugh. But he, too, was very popular at the party.

And lawyers. They also get cornered. If we have a lawyer over, we usually ask another, so they can brief each other. One of our lawyer friends says he wishes he had a nickel for every time someone has inquired, over martinis, "What's the price of a Mexican divorce?"

Just last week, I noticed women huddling around a short, fat man at a big party. So I wondered, what does he have? What's he do? So I asked.

"I'm a big publisher. And secretly everyone has written a book or is going to write one, and they want it published," he said.

"You're kidding. That's just terrible."

"Yes, they accost me at parties, at luncheons, even in men's rooms. I once found a manuscript under a rock on my front porch, and once, at a hotel, under my pillow."

"Do you publish any of these manuscripts?"

"No," he said, "But I'm still looking for another 'Gone With The Wind.'"

"That is incredible," I exclaimed. "By the way, I happen to have this manuscript. Of course, I don't want it published. I just want someone to read it, you understand."

Who Wants To Be First at a Party?

I have this phobia: I can't stand to be the first to arrive at a party.

But my husband can. He likes to be first. If it's a cocktail party at 5, he'll say, "Come on, let's get there at 5 so we can leave at 6 sharp." He's a real party-starter, he is.

I think my mother made me go to birthday parties on time and too early. I was shy. And I can remember sitting alone like a statue in a dark parlor waiting for the Birthday Girl to come downstairs from her nap and bath.

Then a few times, when we've been "on time" at a party, the host and hostess are arguing loudly over who should run out for ice cubes. Or the hostess can't find her left earring and the host is running around barefoot removing the copies of *Playboy* from the coffee table and their unpaid bills from the top of the den desk.

So I always make my husband drive around the block until we at least see two other cars at the party. He's been very good about this procedure. That is until the Doolittles' open house the other night.

The invitations said, "8 to 11." We got there at 8:30 p.m., and there were no cars out front. So we drove around. "Maybe this is the wrong night?" I said.

"I hope so," he answered.

"Look," I yelled, "there are the Mumfords, the Browns, the Martins and Ted and Alice — they are all driving around, too. They don't want to be first either. See."

"Yeah, I see, but we can't stay in this holding pattern too long. Someone has to land first."

"But what will we do in there?"

"Well, we could try talking to each other."

A Little Support Would Be
Helpful in the Calm Before the Party

The 30 minutes before the company comes — it's like the eye of a hurricane, sometimes too calm, and you have nothing left to do. A little on edge, you rearrange the cushions on the sofa for the sixth time. After all, what if the guests forget to come?

I've always said there are two times when a wife expects a husband to be at her side: when she's having a baby and when she's having a party. Funny, isn't it, how some men think both projects are joint ventures, but actually the wife has both?

Now, you would expect your husband to be with you in the kitchen stuffing the cabbage rolls or whipping the mousse, or at least upstairs putting the baby to bed. But no, he has "flown to the store to get some cigarettes." Which only means he had to get out of the house because he couldn't take the pre-party pressure.

Looking back on parties we've given, I guess there are two things I remember best.

One time before a holiday open house he decided to clean out the garage, which not only wasn't necessary (no one goes in the garage during a party, usually), but stirred up a lot of dust and pre-party hostility as well.

The other time he decided the vacuum bag needed changing. He changed it all right. When he turned on the vacuum it spewed out dirt instead of suctioning it, and I had just dusted the entire area.

Often, as I wander through the house checking the ashtrays and the number of forks on the table and to make sure the aspic has molded, he says, "Golly, I forgot the ice." Exit the king.

At least he could tell you that your tan shoes are better with the dress you are wearing than the patent leathers. In other words, give moral support at the last minute. Like "My, but the flowers are lovely."

But no. Five minutes before arrival time, it's "Don't you have any *Harper's* for the coffee table, instead of these dumb *Cosmopolitans*?" Or "Did I tell you Mr. Gretzel is allergic to shellfish?"

Actually, I have found the best and safest thing to do is to leave him tied to a chair in the den with a beer, in front of the 7 o'clock news. Anchor him and close the door.

But the other night I realized what a long way our marriage had come in teamwork. Right before the guests arrived and he was actually counting the toothpicks on the canape tray that was loaded with olives and cheese chunks, he said, "You look absolutely smashing in that. ... That will certainly wow them."

I had just crossed the room barefoot, in a new lacy beige slip. I had not put on my dress yet.

Hold back, don't flip. Your first guest is arriving early.

When the Party is
Harder to Survive than the Year

There must be 50 ways to avoid New Year's Eve parties. I know, I know. Those of you who are young enough to stay up until 4:30 a.m. and sleep until noon — or until the hangover leaves your body — can go ahead and go to your New Year's Eve party. See if I care.

But some of us have had our fill of those traditional parties in big ballrooms, where at midnight you have to kiss the person next to you, who has bad teeth, bad breath, a roving tongue, strong hands and dirty words. You know, the parties where they throw those paper streamers and some obnoxious being toots a tin horn in your ear, and you have to put your arms around everyone and sing "Auld Lang Syne."

I have nothing against celebrating the fact that I have lived another year. What with all the traffic, slippery stairs, faulty car parts, viruses and airborne and bottle-born poisons, it's a darn miracle. So hurray for those of us who made it.

But really, is that any reason to have pre-intimate relations with the stranger next to you at midnight? With all the social diseases on the rampage, is it really expedient to kiss a perfect stranger, anyway? It may not even be healthy to kiss your own husband anymore.

Then there's the other type of party, the one where there are not enough people. These are in somebody's nice, early American, middle-of-the-road home with brass eagles on the wall, baby pictures on the end tables, gardening books on the coffee table and religious needlepoint sayings over the mantle. Because there's not a lot of action, you drink a lot, mixing eggnog with punch and whatever. But just when you want to go somewhere to lie down, like the kitchen floor, the hostess brings out the "finger food:" canapes, dippy dips and little ham slices. (It is not called finger food, by the way, because you can eat it with your fingers. It's because you are so hungry when you leave the party that you have to eat your fingers.)

New Year's Eve party conversations are usually on a level with "Sesame Street," anyway. And there's always one person who has a flair for international politics, and he or she will bore you right into the New Year.

If you simply have to go to a party, avoid such subjects as the MX missile, Social Security and congressional pay raises. Stick instead to banalities, like "What do you do with your poinsettia plants when they stop blooming?"

But it is better still, on New Year's Eve, to go out to eat at a restaurant before 5 in the evening and come home and play Scrabble or paint the den or catch a good movie.

You can risk having the neighbors over for drinks, but only if the time is 4 p.m. That way, they are sure to leave way before midnight. (If they don't, do what Aunt Miranda does with winter guests: Say that you just heard a snow warning.)

And whenever the urge to get out and celebrate the New Year strikes, just remember that Guy Lombardo got paid to stay up past midnight. You won't.

Chapter 3

What's a *Bed* without *Squashed Bananas?*

Ritual at Age 6: Severing Apron Strings

Ever notice that a youngster who used to enjoy splashing in the same bathtub with a brother or a sister, who ran naked out in the back yard at 2 to chase the dog, who let Mommy or Daddy change his diaper or his night shirts, suddenly becomes at 6 a living example of Victorian modesty?

It sure cuts the apron strings where it hurts the most.

When he goes to the bathroom, he locks the door and, I think, may even put a chair up against it. There's no way you could pry him out of there without a hook and ladder. When he undresses at night, he steps into his closet. Or worse, he asks me or his father to turn the other way.

I couldn't find him one morning, he was under his bed covers dressing for school.

Where is the dimpled, freckle-faced darling who would come running to me yelling, "Mom, Mom, a bee has stung me on my seat. Quick, pull the stinger out!"

Where is that lad of 5 who asked me to come into the dressing room of the department store while he tried on different sizes of blue jeans?

I talked about it with a friend of mine who's a psychologist, "Oh, it's perfectly natural, just a stage," was the reply. "He's found out he's a boy."

"And he doesn't think I know?" I said.

"No, he knows you know, and he doesn't want to discuss it openly. Maybe you all should walk around more casually, with fewer clothes on. He's growing up, but he needs to know there's nothing to hide. Why, kids play naked in the fountains in Sweden until they are 10 or 11."

""Well, I can't afford to take him to Sweden," I declared.

"Buy him a fountain then, one you could all use."

Phooey on psychologists.

Peers Pale Beside Supermom

The Supermom at Christmas time. I don't hate her. I just envy her.

At holiday time, she not only manages to serve willingly on all church decorating committees, but also keeps up with her four car pools, puts in her storm windows herself and has an open house for 100 people, at which she looks ravishing in her handmade felt Christmas skirt. She makes all her Christmas presents, and to top everything, she doesn't get the flu after it's all over.

Last year, Supermom constructed doll beds from old bleach bottles, braided spaghetti into Christmas wreaths, made 7-foot candles from her mother-in-law's left over bacon grease, made corn husk dolls and four dozen napkin rings from baked bread dough.

And this year to make me feel all the more schlumpy, she's making Barbie doll tea sets from acorns and walnut shells.

Worse than what Supermom can do is what I read in the December family magazines, like "32 ways to brighten your Christmas with homemade gifts."

These articles tell you "what you can do, in no time at all ..."

Which is what I have, no time at all.

One magazine suggest using old doorknobs to fashion small figures for a crèche (funny, but I'm just fresh out of doorknobs); sequined covers for toilet paper rolls (our toilet paper goes so fast there's not time to cover it); a seashell mobile made from seashells you've collected over the years (only I haven't); and doll houses out of cigar boxes (we don't smoke).

Actually, all this creativity has just made me consider making Christmas tree ornaments from old dust balls that I find under my son's bed.

And, oh, how the Supermom can cook at Christmas! Before you can say "turkey," she has made 12 sugar plum fairy cakes, four dozen minced meat lucia tarts and 22 praline-bottomed pumpkin pies.

In the past few years, my only contribution toward an old-timey Christmas is hauling the Christmas tree into the living room from the car while I hum carols, changing the light bulbs on the front porch to red from white and putting a green bow on the dog's collar.

But someday when I am retired, I will set aside time to make four pounds of rum balls for each of my friends, lace them and me with a little bourbon and whistle while I work.

Sibling Rivalry Relieved
with that Gift Gambit

Having difficulty with sibling rivalry at your house? In our family, we licked the problem by having new babies give gifts as well as receive them.

I mean that when we brought a new member of the family home from the hospital, we also brought presents for the other children marked "from your new brother (or sister)." In fact, this worked so well that the kids were always hounding me to go back to the hospital and have another baby — like every week.

I'm not saying we never had any difficulties with sibling rivalry, but it wasn't exactly a household word. I tended to ignore it unless it was accompanied by high fever or bleeding.

In case you haven't experienced it at your house, sibling rivalry is when your 2-year-old says to you, "Mom, why can't the stork come take the new baby back?"

Or when two children are fighting on top of the piano over a piece of bubblegum you gave the younger one for walking the dog.

Myrtle up the street had the problem so badly at her house she had to set the kitchen timer and clock for each child's time with toys, bikes or grandmother.

A friend of mine, a psychologist, had a new strategy, but it backfired.

When she brought her new baby home from the hospital, she handed her 3-year-old son a doll complete with diapers, pins and bottles and said, "Here, darling, here's your very own baby."

Two weeks later, she discovered that the 3-year-old had stuck pins in the doll, cut off its hair and banished it to eternal darkness in the closet.

So the family threw the doll away and bought a Great Dane for the boy.

Cliche Adult Reactions to New Baby

What makes adults act like infants when they see a new baby?

Even the most staid grownup seems overcome by an urge to shake, jiggle, rattle and roll and "cootchie-coo" the new arrival under the chin. The adult may gurgle more than the baby.

I'm so glad a Pittsburgh pediatrician has come out with evidence that a whole lot of shakin', even in a loving manner, can harm an infant.

Good for that pediatrician.

Now, maybe some of our adoring grandparents and aunts and uncles will let the Juniors of the world get some rest.

Let sleeping dogs lie, I've always said. In fact, I used to put a sign on the baby's crib, "If you wake him, you have to feed him." Kind of like at the zoo.

I was also a germ-a-maniac with the first baby. I gave everyone who came in to peek over the edge of the bassinet a mask. It also muffled their voices.

I would love to ask that pediatrician if the dumb things people say and do in front of the new baby also could have a lasting effect.

For example:

"Why, he looks just like Jim; he has his eyes." And then you have to tell them the baby is adopted.

"Whose red hair does he have — the milkman, ha, ha?' Old, stale joke.

"My, she's big for 3 months." And she is only 3 weeks old.

"Oh, isn't she beautiful." And she's a boy.

"Look at all those dimpled rings of fat; aren't they darling?" The baby's been on a diet for two months.

"Bet she'll break a lot of hearts when she gets older." Old cliche.

"What little fingers he has for a boy baby." As the speaker winds his dirty fingers around the newborn's germ-free, clean ones.

"Oh, so you're bottle feeding the baby? I always …" You know the rest.

Perhaps the best thing to say when viewing a newborn is just what an old maid aunt of mine used to declare: "Well, it's a baby."

What's a Bed Without Squashed Bananas?

A bed of my own? (or things I have slept with): Sounds crazy doesn't it, but I know it's impossible in my lifetime — a bed of my own! I even have this recurring dream in which I am buried, and I have to share the coffin.

To me, a bed is a very important thing — it is the alpha and the omega, the beginning of life and the end. For me, the bed is one of my favorite things.

But I have wondered what it would be like to have a king-size bed, all my own with satin-paisley sheets, and an electric blanket that made morning coffee and orange juice, too. I grew up sleeping with a dog and two cats, and sometimes a little sister who got cold in the night. I got married and shared a bed. I had four children and not only shared my bed, but I also was pushed out at times.

Let's talk about the bed. I've slept with a plastic aircraft carrier, eight crumbled graham crackers, a role of scotch tape, one wet-diapered 2-year-old, one feverish 5-year-old and a newborn guinea pig who was whimpering.

But they may take the bed away, the established bed anyway. They have taken away food we like. They may take the car away and replace it with the horse and buggy, and now they dare to tamper with the bed.

Albert and Ginny Sloth have a new waterbed. It weights 1,700 pounds when full and holds 200 gallons of water. It takes one and a half hours to fill up, and you can just attach a garden hose to the bed and fill it up. You can get one from $140 to $250, but they've had some trouble.

Like when Fat Albert turns over quickly in his sleep, he bounces skinny Ginny right out onto the floor. Then when I was over there last, they were having a violent argument over the fact that Albert needed to cut his toenails, and Ginny was yelling, "If you trip over that hose one more time, I'll cut off your water."

Just about anybody or anything has landed next to me in the night in my co-op bed. We have some unspoken rules: like a child has to have had a really bad nightmare and be over 5 to climb in with us, and his or her fever has to be above 101 degrees. They must also crawl in next to the mother, because once the father woke up and yelled, "There's a squashed banana under me." I yelled back, "No, it's just a wet sock — go back to sleep." But in the morning, we noticed it was a squashed banana without the peel.

I even remembered one stormy night on a vacation trip in the tropics, or was it Ocean City? — when I was trying to decide whose bed I could hide in, when four little children, two dolls and one Linus blanket crept into our bed. It was just too crowded, so I decided we would all sleep across the bed for maximum room. Have you ever tried to move a sleeping giant without waking him? All he said the next morning was, "We could stand a new bed. This one is getting too short."

There are certain sources that are trying to downgrade the family in America, but please don't let them take the bed away.

Now, if they take the bed out of the family or the family out of the bed — they may take the fun out of life. Right?

My Baby's Better than Your Baby

"You mean Pammy does not sleep through the night yet? My Jenny did at 4 weeks."

"Isn't Dodie on meat yet? Golly, Mary was on meat at 3 weeks."

"You mean to tell me you still have to put Igor on the potty before he goes to bed? That must be exhausting. Jerry's been dry at night for two months."

On and on it goes: the baby-brag litany. From coast to coast and boast to boast the one-upmanship rages.

The "whose-baby-is-best game" is played from incubator to high chair. It takes place at Tupperware or cocktail parties or checkout lines at supermarkets or car washes. It is played at an exceptionally high pitch in pediatricians' offices.

I remember sitting in the doctor's office with a 6-month-old baby in my lap when a woman with a crying baby in her lap turned to me and said, "Doesn't she crawl? Harriet crawls."

And she put Harriet on the floor and Harriet crawled, still screaming. I couldn't put my baby on the floor because the floor was dirty. So I said to her, "It's amazing that Harriet crawls so fast, when she is so, uh, fat" (hitting below the belt).

"No, Harriet was 12 pounds at birth. She's not really fat, that's muscle and she's crying because she wants to walk."

"That's wonderful," I said, giving up the game.

Just yesterday, I overheard two mothers with babies on their backs talking in the supermarket over by the hams.

"Isn't Jenny weaned?"

"No, my doctor believes in nursing as long as we can."

"Well, Billy does suck his thumb still. We don't know how to break him of that habit, but he is potty trained. At least I don't have to do diapers anymore."

"Jenny never sucked her thumb, and she can eat with a spoon now."

And on and on it went, until I couldn't stand it. I went up to them.

"What darling babies," I said. "I'll bet you will hate it when they grow up and you have to worry about how fast they are going in the car and which college they can get in. Count your blessings now."

"You mean things don't get better?" one asked.

"Oh no. Later on, you just compare things like acne medications or SAT scores. And you two must remember you've never seen a teen-ager in diapers or a college student who has to drink milk out of a bottle."

And as I drove my shopping cart out of sight, one of them called to me, "But have you ever seen a bride coming down the aisle who sucked her thumb?"

"No, but I bet there are some who have wanted to," I answered with my thumb in my mouth and a smile on my lips.

The Normal Cycle of Being a Mother

Some mothers are remembered for their smiles, their sponge cakes, their gravy, their storytelling, their needlepoint, their excellent car-pooling, their tempers or their keen understanding.

But not this one. I will be remembered for "La Machine." The washing machine.

Let me explain. Now that the four children are grown and have left home, temporarily anyway (never bolt the door for good), I have tried very hard to cut the umbilical cord. I try not to dictate to them, but just to be there when I am needed.

After all, I don't have to cook, sew or care for them anymore, so I keep a low disciplinary profile.

But I find I am needed now more than at any other time for my washing machine.

First, it was the college kid who came home for a weekend.

"Oh, what's in those brown paper sacks, dear?" I asked, hoping it was corn on the cob he had just picked along the way.

"Well, Mom, just a few dirty things here and there. Actually, it's two weeks' laundry. I just didn't have the quarters to go to the laundromat."

Then along comes the college senior with the apartment.

"Mom, do you mind if I do some laundry while I'm here? Sue Ellen and I didn't have time to go to a washateria. We are having finals. You know how it is … and we washed at her folks' last month."

Then came the young marrieds, coming home for a holiday.

"My, you brought so much baggage for such a short time," I comment stupidly.

"Mom, I hope you don't mind. The laundromat is so far from our place, and we were in a hurry to get here…"

Then just last weekend while I was waiting for a train, a young man with three full duffle bags was sitting next to me.

"Being reassigned? Going overseas, I guess?" I ask pleasantly.

"Well, uh, no, actually I'm going home. I'm taking my laundry. I just didn't have time before I left and my mother's machine has a great wash' n 'wear cycle. I guess your kids wouldn't do that, huh?"

"Heavens no," I lied.

But I wanted to tell him the truth that on my tombstone may be inscribed one of the following epitaphs:

"Here lies Mom, who had the fastest washing machine in the East." Or "Here lies gullible Mom, who thought we washed our clothes between our visits home."

Or maybe they'll bury me with my washing machine as in the ancient Egyptian style, and the marker will just state simply: "La Machine — the only thing that could run 'cycles' around our Mom."

Chapter 4

Car-Caged Animals

The Car Pooler's Highest Echelon

You have not risen to the highest echelon of car poolery until you've driven six 5-year-old ballerinas to their dancing class.

I was a substitute car pool mother last week and had to pick up and deliver a bevy of would-be dancers to Mr. Camille's studio.

The first child I picked up was to tell me where the next child lived. But I found out something — a 5-year-old child doesn't always know where the others live. Like an Eagle Scout, each youngster tried to help by telling me at which tree or bush to turn, or "I think that's Pam's house: she has a white poodle."

We had to wait at least 8 1/2 minutes at each house, because one ballerina forgot to put her hair in a pony tail, something Mr. Camille demanded; one would-be dancer tripped on a skateboard on the way out to the car; one forgot to go to the bathroom before getting into her leotard; one put her pink tights on backward and one cried because she wanted to play football with her brother instead of going to ballet.

I was given the option once I got to Mr. C's studio to either wait with the other mothers for an hour or go shopping. I took one look at the young mothers, who were already talking about diapers, recipes and other car pools, and decided I didn't even have the energy to talk.

Instead, I chose to sit behind the wheel of the car, doze a little and fantasize. ...

I wondered, of the six kids, would there really be one who would ever make the chorus line of the high school performance of "Nutcracker Suite"? I wondered when, or if any would ever learn where each of the others lived, at least while I was car pooling. And I wondered, as other car pool mothers have I'm sure, was this trip really necessary?

Mom Hep With 'Go-Withs'

Do you know what a "to go with" is?

Well, if you're the parents of anyone from maybe 11 to 24, you'd better get with it and find out.

This is how it came up. Phyllis, who has four teen-agers — and a degree in psychology, thank goodness — told us at the bridge club that Trixie, her 12-year-old, had just turned down an invite "to go with" the captain of the football team at her junior high.

"I'm so proud of her for doing this, because all her friends go with someone, you know," Phyllis said.

"So kids still go steady today?" I asked.

"Oh, no," she replied. "They don't call it that. They use the term 'go with.' A girl or boy has a go-with. Where have you been?"

"Gee," I went on, "I can remember in my day we called it a 'boyfriend' and my mother called it a 'beau' and my father said, 'a sweetheart.'"

"Yeah," Phyllis said ruefully. "They don't even get pinned anymore or engaged. It's not half as much fun as our day, and the girls don't get the car door opened for them either."

Yes, we have go-withs at our house (I didn't want to be outdone by Phyllis). But my kids are weird, I guess. Most of them "went with" me, until they got to be at least 14.

"Just think," I told my friends, "in our day, you never had just one boyfriend (excuse the expression). You collected as many boyfriends as you could. I mean, the more boys you dated the more popular you were. Right?"

Phyllis explained that although she is proud to have a kid who broke the system, she thinks go-withs are a good thing. "Because it doesn't commit them to anything, no ring, no pin, no corsages."

"Do you have to marry a go-with?" someone asked Phyllis.

"No, but you must not go out with anyone else, and there are some do's and don'ts, such as don't use the word date. And don't ask your go-with, 'Did you see that cute new boy at the filling station the other day?' That's a no-no."

"They just say, 'Oh, mother,' or worse, 'Yuk.'"

Then I finally asked the real nitty-gritty question: "Can you live with a go-with?" I wanted to know what to expect.

"Yes, you can," Phyllis explained, "but that's really called 'living with.' I mean, you say, Ann Brown is living with Joe Smith. A live-with is a night and day thing, a sort of in-depth go-with."

"OK, I think I've got it. I'm going right home now and talk to the kids and find out who's going with whom and any other things I should know.

"And then I think I'll ask my husband for an old-fashioned date this very night."

Car-Caged Animals

There are certain things you discover about people during long hot car trips that would only surface during a ride in a small space shuttle or a lay-over in a powerless elevator.

As prepared as you may be for a car vacation with human beings, you find there is animal in everyone:

- That children A,B, C and D like to hear rock music on the car radio all day and all night.
- That the father must hear the baseball game even while driving through Oklahoma in a thunderous cloudburst.
- That the mother wants to hear the weather as often as possible.
- That favorite programs fade when you get out-of-range of the local station, and it's hard to explain that to a 4-year-old.
- That children do not play "see how many out-of-state licenses we can count" anymore. They want a portable TV and a full set of Legos for the car.
- That children B and D can consume 12 bottles of soda pop between the Pennsylvania and Ohio turnpikes without any stops, but that children A and C have weak bladders.
- That A and C can sleep sitting up all day in a car, but then they can't sleep in the motel at night.
- That the favorite exercise of B and C while sitting in the back seat is kicking the back of the front seat while the driver tries to figure out where Exit 12 went.
- That air conditioning in the car makes A and C sneeze continuously. And that C gets sunburned through the car windows and her running shorts.

- That almost no one can fold a road map correctly in a moving car.
- That the fried chicken Aunt Sadie packed for the trip does turn soggy after two hours and that plums and peaches do not ripen in a few hours in the front seat.
- That conversations are not on a high level, even though the parents try. Such things as "whoever gets in the motel first to break the paper sanitary ribbon across the toilet seat gets to pick the side of the bed on which he sleeps" can be a four- to five-hour harangue.
- That someday A, B, C and D will grow up to like long car trips, but that mostly they'll just grow up.

It's Never Too Late to Flunk

What do you do if you're a dropout from "parent-testing"? I'm getting a little embarrassed about all the parent tests in women's magazines that I have failed.

According to them, I should have dropped out of marriage and parenting long ago. My scores are always zilch.

You know the kinds of tests I mean. They scream out at you from the cover of the slick mags — "Do You Really Love Your Kids?" "Do Your Children Run Your Home?" Then inside they have a little quiz to make you a better parent or tell you there's no hope.

In a recent issue of a national magazine, there is a test written by a doctor and titled "How Well Are You Doing As A Parent?"

I failed each of the 12 questions, even with multiple choices.

Sample question: If your 4-year-old screams and carries on, creating a disturbance in a grocery store because he wants a candy bar — what do you do?

I will delete my expletive.

The magazine's answer: "Ignore him. Ignoring someone, especially in public, is crucial to the future reduction of such disruption."

I'm sorry, but if every parent ignored every child who screams in a supermarket, no one would shop and then no one would eat.

I wonder if the doctor has ever had three screaming kids hanging onto a careening shopping cart, fighting over two M&Ms that have slipped to the floor?

Another question: The teacher told you your child was caught throwing spitballs. What should you do?

The magazine gives this answer: "Parents should confide in their child their own naughty past to establish an easy flow of communication with Mom and Dad. …"

Well, I can't go along with that one either. First, I didn't know kids were still making spitballs, and, if so, are they that bad? And wow, would you really want your kids to know some of the things you did in school? Spitballs would be considered benign.

Anyway, having given all the wrong answers, I'm pondering certain choices in my future: a) give up mothering and let the kids take over, b) give up mothering and let my husband take over or c) give up taking tests in women's magazines.

First Pinstripe Suit: It's Worn With Cleats

There's nothing like that first baseball uniform. When the coach finally gives them their uniforms, the level of accomplishment and pride lies somewhere between the first time he said, "Da Da" and the day he learned to ride a two-wheeler.

He stood in front of the mirror, smiling triumphantly. "It has stripes, too," he said.

Nothing fit, but he didn't notice, and we pretended we didn't either. The pants were gathered at the waist with one of my old belts. The shirt was so huge that the décolletage outdid Cher's. The cap came so far down on his ears that only earrings would have stopped it from covering his entire head. And the socks had large holes in them and parts of them were missing.

The uniform and accessories cost $17, and that's only rented. You give everything back at the end of the season.

"Yeah, but I get to keep the hat forever," he said, "and those aren't holes, Mom, they are just real baseball socks; they're like stirrups."

"Oh, no," I said, "what I see are huge lumps — someone has mended them."

"Well, you can't have everything. I don't mind running on rocks," and he smiled again. "Remember we have to keep the uniform clean at all times, they're wash 'n' wear, the coach said."

"Thank goodness for modern technology," I exclaimed.

"Oh, Mom, one more thing, will you buy two quarts of beef stew for $3, or would you like an apron for a dollar in the team's colors? We need the money for transportation for the away games."

"Who made the stew and the aprons, not the same mothers who mended the socks?" I asked.

He answered with all the candor of the 9-year-old. "Some nice mothers, who love to cook and sew. ..."

"That's OK, that's OK. Here's 10 bucks, and tell those supermoms your mother's a vegetarian who doesn't wear aprons. But she loves baseball, and kids ... and she can drive in a car pool."

Mother's Hour Is a Laugh

No wonder I'm a raving maniac, and you may be, too, if you have school-children who are yours living in your house.

When the dishes are done, and the house becomes quiet, comes a pause in the day's occupation that is known as the "mother's hour." That's a laugh. I mean, every evening when the day is done, I think, now we will have our quiet time.

I will sit in a slinky lounging outfit, with long earrings, my feet up on the coffee table in front of the television and my husband at my side.

We will talk over the day or maybe the next 10 years during the commercials. But let me tell you how it really is.

A typical week. Somewhere between 7 p.m. and 10 p.m.:

MONDAY — High school student: "Mom, Mom, I'm making a comparison between Assyro-Babylonian mythology and Egyptian mythology. Do you know anything about it? I need it right away." (Does she realize the only myth I am familiar with is the one which leads me to believe I can have a quiet evening at home?)

TUESDAY — Junior high student: "Mother, I'm making a sculpture of a man balancing on his right index finger, and I need a picture to go by. Do we have a picture like that?" (No, but would you believe I tried to pose for it?)

WEDNESDAY — Sixth grader: "Mom, quick, I'm writing a paper on the koala bear and its feeding habits."

"Please, why did you take such a narrow subject?"

"Mom, I was absent the day they gave out subjects, and that was the only one left." (We ran to the library by way of the zoo.)

THURSDAY — Third grader: "Mom, I need all the instruction labels out of your synthetic dresses for social studies." (We cut the labels out of all two of my synthetic dresses and then I had to worry about the teacher's "social" explanation on why some of the mothers have only two synthetic dresses and some have 10 ... but I told him to tell the teacher I have four permapress tablecloths.)

FRIDAY — Oh, joy, I say to myself, it's Friday night and there's no homework for tomorrow, and my husband and I are sitting in front of an open fire — in the house, that is.

"Mom, I forgot to tell you my Sunday school teacher says we have to make a relief map out of flour and water of the city of Atlantis."

An answer: "We're out of flour and the water in the well has dried up, and so did the city of Atlantis, as a matter of fact."

Chapter 5

Mom-Schooling

A Chore Mother Hates: Sandwiches at 6 a.m.

Premise: Some housewives like all their chores (some housewives are crazy); a few housewives like some of their chores (some are not so crazy). Conclusion: I like a few of my household chores, (I'm really normal?).

But there are two chores I hate: ironing and making sack lunches for school at 6 a.m. on a rainy Monday morning.

There is just no way to get out of this chore, unless you are rich enough to let all four kids eat at school, but then you'll have one sparrow-eater who says the "school stuff stinks."

Guess last year was one of my worst years. As I staggered into the kitchen with my disheveled hair, eyebrows and nightgown, I plugged in the coffee and news, hoping one would combat the other, then I made: ONE pressed ham and cheese on rye with no crusts and one chocolate Tasty Kake thrown in; ONE crunchy peanut butter and jelly on white with crusts and one chocolate Tasty Kake thrown in; ONE creamy peanut butter and jelly with one Tasty Pie — for the acne-prone boy child!

To any steeplejack working on a high rise on the swing shift, this sandwiching, I guess, would look like a pretty good job. But try it, you'll hate it.

Can you really discern in the dark of a winter morning between the labels "crunchy" or "creamy"? Both have six letters, right?

Would you believe that there was an 18-day school stretch when the management had the flu and certain P.B. sandwiches got mixed up. Those nasty, spoiled kids traded their sandwiches when they got the wrong P.B.s. they traded for baseball cards, records and money — they didn't eat lunch.

Can a mother's contract be broken for giving a kid the wrong P.B.?

But last week was my worst one.

You see, I place the lunches in the refrigerator and I put each child's initial on the sack until they are ready to fly out the door. The kid, that is. But somebody took my sack of Jerusalem artichokes, which I love (a neighbor had just given them to me from his farm), to school, instead of lunch.

Later: "What did you do with them? You didn't eat them, I hope?"

"No, Mom, I yelled 'Who wants to buy some tulip bulbs?' — that's what I thought they were — and then I thought I'd use the dough to buy a hot lunch. ..."

"So?"

"Well, Mom, some smart kid said, 'Hey, those are Jerusalem artichokes — I'll buy them.' Then he ate them."

"He ate them? Raw?"

"Yeah, he's hipped on that Earth food and transcendental mediation — all that bag, you know. He's only 15 and he had a beard, too."

"Didn't you see that I'd marked 'AC' on the sack?"

"Yeah, I wondered why you'd forgotten my name again."

Just Pick a Couple of Grand

I hope you teachers out there have had a nice summer and will be kind to your students' parents.

I mean, do you teachers realize what you do to us those first few weeks of school, especially between the hours of 3 and 11 p.m.?

For example: school supplies: "Oh, no, I have to have the notebook paper with five holes in it, Mom."

"Mom, Miss Zilch says I have to have three art gum erasers and two cigar boxes by tomorrow."

"Mom, I need 23 plastic margarine cups by next week."

"Mom, I need three empty Clorox bottles by Wednesday."

"Mom, I need a slide rule by tomorrow."

"Mom, I need to make some homemade paste by Thursday."

"Mom, the coach says I need new tennis shoes, I have a hole in one."

"Mom, can you start making 15 pilgrim hats by November 1?"

Hypothesis: "Listen, kids, you know that money tree we have growing out back, well, just go on out there and pick a couple of grand off the limbs and take what you need for school. Give the teacher some, too. Because I'm too busy with my new course, 'Yoga At Home,' with Dr. No-How."

'We Won't Cry, Will We?' as the Door Slams

There's a real soap opera episode in your life when you leave your baby at the school door. I was never quite prepared, nor were the teachers prepared for me.

Here's this cherub that you've borne, nursed, nurtured into childhood, only to be snatched away from you forever by the school system.

Am I kidding? I know some bridge- and golf-playing mothers who contemplate all summer their September freedom. At the end of the summer, they unchain their kids and drive them to school with a whip.

Seriously, though, if you're a Bobbsey Twin-type mother you have built first grade up all summer long. You've told him how lovely his teacher will be and what fun it will be to learn that "Jack and Jane have a dog named Spot."

There are several kinds of first-grade teachers. There's one who meets you at the door (your first-grader is clinging to your moist hand) and says, "Oh, and how are we? Now, we're not going to cry are we?" Did she mean me? Bobby's face, which had been happy until he heard that, screwed up. He cried.

Then there's the type who says, "Now, mother, you must go shopping. The bus will bring him home — we are going to be fine."

With that, Bobby, who always went shopping with me and loved every counter at the market, really started crying.

I thought at least she could ask me to go home in case she had to call. Little did she know that I'd be hiding in the bushes outside the schoolroom waiting for him to cry "Mama."

Then there's the type of teacher who has never taught. She's fresh out of college. She's young, pretty and her upper lip is trembling.

When she sees Bobby crying, she whispers, "Would you stay in the hall or in the bathroom until I get him quiet." This type instills instant fear in your heart, and you pray that the teacher matures before the bell rings.

Then there's the type of old maid teacher who has been teaching for years and she can hardly stand to think of another season with 30 unruly kids.

She takes one look at you from top to bottom, and, like the head nurse on the OB floor says, "Just follow me, please, quietly and quickly, we don't want to be late." Somehow, they follow this type. She doesn't smile, but kids sense that she is the commander.

The door of the first grade is the place that separates the softies from the hardies, the bad mothers from the good mothers and the bad teachers from the good teachers.

I didn't cry much. I ran home to defrost the refrigerator, get out the winter clothes, paint his closet and talk on the phone uninterruptedly. But I was just doing the breakfast dishes when I heard a small voice say, "Mama, I'm home."

School was over — it was noon. I ran to him to check him for bruises, missing buttons — to see if all his limbs were intact. He made it.

"Was the bus fun, darling?"

"No."

"Was school nice?"

"No."

"You didn't cry, did you?"

"No, but the teacher did all day."

"Didn't you just love your teacher?"

"No."

"I bet you can't wait to go back."

"No."

"Well, did you miss Mommy, dear?"

"Nope."

So I guess we're going to be OK.

When the Children Grow Up and Have All the Answers

It's a funny thing. You send your children off to college or they leave home to get married, and you expect them to change. But I've been noticing something: They come back — and they try to change you.

In other words, it's a role reversal thing. Suddenly, they are the knowing ones, the parental figures. I mean, they know more about the world from their textbooks, and they even have better recipes for chicken soup. Suddenly, they seem to know what's better for you, their aging parents.

Two of them ganged up on me while home recently.

"Mom, you must get some new clothes," she said, leafing through my closet full of treasures collected since the 1940s.

"Your polyester dress and stretch pants all have to go. They have snags. Here, let us help you."

"Well, just call me the poly kid," I said flippantly. "I love polyester."

"No," she said sternly. "You should stick to linen, cottons and silks — natural fibers."

"But you don't understand. Natural fibers stick to me. In fact, they wrinkle, crinkle and have to be ironed. I threw my iron away in 1969. I just press your father's handkerchief inside the encyclopedia."

So the two queens of natural fiber — or were they Army generals? — marched into the kitchen.

"We've gone through the fridge, Mom, and it's full of sugar and salty food! You and Dad will just feel better if you cut out salt and sugar."

"But I feel better now that your father and I don't eat rich desserts or bread for dinner."

"You don't understand, Mom. There's sugar in your mayonnaise and in some of your frozen dinners and your Rice Krispies. We've put some tofu — it's protein — and yogurt in here."

When they were combing the fridge, they spotted the liquor shelf.

"Who drinks all this?" they gasped, as if they had discovered a cache of cocaine.

"We don't, " I said. "It's for friends who drop by. I just have a drink before dinner some nights. Gee, I don't smoke ..."

"Mom, just stick to white wine and throw away the bourbon," they urged.

Well, the inquisition ended amicably. We went out the next day and bought one cotton suit, one silk blouse and $55 worth of food at a health food store, which I could have bought at a chain store for $25. And I treated them to ice cream sundaes while they weren't looking.

But I told them, "Look, girls, I'll do anything to look younger and be what you want me to be. But remember, you've got to give us time. It'll take a while to learn to like bean sprout sandwiches. After all, I gave you time to like Gerber's strained spinach."

When they pulled out of sight, I slammed the door and ran and jumped into my polyester slacks and acrylic sweater and got out my last box of Rice Krispies.

The Rewards of Being Good and Fat

She was sitting next to her mother, watching her brother play softball. And the mother said, "I know you are bored, Maggie. Why don't you go see what they have to drink over there? And on the way home I will buy you a chocolate milk shake."

The child said yes, she was bored, and yes, she could hardly wait to get a milk shake, but she also wanted a hot dog. "Well, we just had supper, but you have had to sit a long time," her mother agreed.

Maggie looked about 10, but she was already fat.

At the restaurant the other day, a child next to me was fidgeting because the service was slow, and his mother said, "Let's see if I can get you an ice cream cone first as it looks like the dinner is going to take a long time. ... It was nice of you to come with us." This child, too, was plump.

And once we were driving on an interstate, and my friend's 14-year-old started complaining about having to go along. My friend said, "Julie, look, as soon as you see a McDonald's, we'll stop, OK? You watch out for one. Meantime, open my tote bag and grab one of those chocolate bars. (We'd just had breakfast.) I know how it is to be young and bored with all this adult talk." Julie is also fat.

What's going on? I don't know about you, but I'm seeing a lot of fat children lately. It seems that food has become the reward for good behavior.

Take my friend Jane. She went to work two years ago, and her 6-year-old son had to come home from school to an empty house every day. But he could eat anything he wanted while looking at television. Jane says he drinks about six soda pops a day. And he is now a fat 8-year-old.

Haven't we learned that soft drinks have too much sugar and that some have caffeine? We also know that fatty foods and too much sugar are bad for children. But some parents are going right along with the "behave and get a treat" reward system.

As a mother, I was guilty of bribing my children, too, but I didn't do it with food. I remember telling one child, "I will give you $1 for each 'A' you get next semester." And I did.

I asked Harvey Rapp, a clinical psychologist in Columbia, about this trend toward food rewards.

"It's a reverse form of behavior management," he said. "The effect of the food reward is only immediate, and it accomplishes what you are looking for, maybe. But in the long run, you can build in wrong behavior and certainly a process of weight gain.

"It's kind of putting the cart before the horse. We are reinforcing the whining or misbehavior by promising food. Hence, there could be a spiraling effect.

"Children who are left alone in the afternoon should be involved in some afternoon program. There should be some contingency plan to keep these children from eating and looking at TV. Food is a primary reinforcement. However, we use behavior management for special education or when there is a self-destructive pattern with a child. I find that behavior management programs are very helpful in very specific problems or when a child is self-destructive."

Then again, the psychologist said, laughing, "You know maybe this overeating among kids is due to the fad diet craze. We do talk an awful lot about food, don't we?"

So "Eat and shut up" or "Eat and be good" is not just one mother's imagination.

BankaMothercard Was Really Dreamy

Ever heard of BankaMothercard? (Every mother should have one.)
Well, neither had I, until I had this dream the other night.

In the dream, I'd just filled up with gasoline at the filling station and I opened my purse to give the man $10, and I found only $1.18. I said, apologetically, "That's what happens when you have borrowing teen-agers. They clean you out."

He didn't laugh, but before he could yell "police," I heard this loud ring.

It was my pocketbook, it had turned into a computer bank. And out the side flap came a credit card, then a voice. "Here is your BankaMothercard. Just rub your fingers over the correct digits, put your card into slot A, located on the other side of your pocketbook and the desired amount of money will come out."

It worked and I gave the service station man his money with a smile.

How great. I could hardly wait to get home and tell the kids. Life was going to be a bowl of money. I might even lend my BankaMothercard to those kids I live with. It was like having an Aladdin's lamp.

Because in real life and before my dream, I would start the week out with, say $30, and then it was, "Mom, OK if I borrow 3 bucks from you for our history teacher's flowers? I'll put an IOU in your purse."

Or: "Mom, I took 25 cents out of your purse for the neighborhood 'Kill-The-Rats-Drive.' The lady came by and needed a donation."

Or: "Mom, I'm sorry, but last night after you were asleep, I had to take $10 out of you pocketbook for my gym suit. The teacher said if we didn't have the money in by tomorrow, we'd have to go naked. I'll pay you back when Joe Smith pays me back." And on it went.

So by Friday lunchtime, I would have 89 cents in my change purse and two bobby pins.

Well, in the dream, things were different. All I had to do was insert my BankaMothercard in the slot, and out came money, money, money.

However, sometimes when I asked for too much money, an alarm sounded and the voice said, "Does not compute" or "Advance to another loan source" or "Go to jail."

But toward the end of the dream, quite foolishly, clutching my beloved BankaMothercard, I went to another bank and tried to get a loan to take a four-month cruise.

The woman at the bank looked like one of my kid's teachers, and she said, "Sorry, lady, but we don't honor this card. In fact, I've never seen one like this."

Then I cried out and screamed, "Mother, mother." And I woke up. My husband claims I was yelling, "Money, money!"

You Can't Get Even with 'Odd' Children

Women with an even number of children have it made. All things edible can be divided in half. But when you have to divide things into thirds or fifths — especially a round object, a pear, a kumquat — it's the pits. It's tough. I was never any good at fractions or division anyway.

Why is it kids who don't want to set the table or who won't help you peel a potato will watch you like an FBI agent when you are dividing ice cream or two chocolate cookies into five shares?

I have popped the 13th jelly bean into my overstuffed mouth rather than divide it three ways, and so have you if you have "uneven" children and want to avoid war.

Just the other day I was dividing the remaining Coke for five small children. Their eyes never left my hands, the silence was so great you could have heard a bubble drop to the kitchen floor, until one hollered, "Jimmy got more. ..."

I had made the mistake of using see-through drinking glasses, so there was a rumble from the hawk-eyed malcontents.

I got a teaspoon and shifted some of the Coke. Then someone else yelled out, "It's still not even."

Then I got an eyedropper, because there was a mutiny forming, and kitchens have a lot of loose weaponry hanging around.

And why is it a child who hates pumpkin bread screams if he gets three crumbs fewer than his sister, who also hates pumpkin bread? And don't ever divide with a dull knife. In fact, if you have a slide rule, a funnel, syringe and a measuring tape, you are safer in the kitchen.

The other night, I was pouring chocolate milk into paper cups on the kitchen table for what used to be five nice children. Until one of them told me that one leg of the kitchen table was shorter, and I'd have to pour again. I got so mad that I poured the stuff back into the pitcher and got five straws, and said, "OK, the kid with the most mouth power will finish first — divide and conquer."

Using Psychology 101, when you want three children who hate peas to eat them, simply place four peas on one plate and 14 on the other and two half-peas on the third. This way they will fight over the peas, and sometimes, eat each pea. The nutritional value of half a pea is better than no pea at all.

No Rest for the Weary Mom

In case your daughter isn't yet 6-, 7- or even 10-years-old, I feel I should prepare you for something that's as popular and as nerve-racking as the skateboard: It's the "slumber party."

Now, they aren't exactly new, but they have reached an all-time peak in some areas. Like "Star Wars," they are the "in-est" thing with the "teeney-est" set.

They must have started in covered-wagon days, when whole families descended on you in the summer while migrating across the country. They spread quilts on the floor, all 20 of them, on a hot summer night. And you never knew how long they were going to stay.

Now, slumber parties are a social phenomenon or maybe a sport. Some behaviorists think their resurgence came in with the sale of these cutesy sleeping bags for tiny tots. You know, they're printed with colorful clowns or cats.

These new bags zip up, but they don't cover the head area and so they don't hold in the noise. I repeat, they do not cover the mouth, so there's absolutely no acoustical control.

I know an 8-year-old who had 16 slumber parties to go to during the holidays. Apparently everytime there is a birthday party in her age group, they have a slumber party. But, let me tell you, they never sleep.

My neighbor, Pam, 30, who just underwent a slumber party and spent 10 days at a rest spa, says the slumber party is the cheapest kind of birthday party. You don't have to furnish any entertainment or prizes, and the children don't even care about celebrating a birthday. They giggle and bring their own records. Sleep isn't a big thing.

Pam tells me, "If you are a stalwart parent, you can have as many as 20 kids and feed them a brief carryout supper — maybe a basket of Big Macs, soda pop and, later on, popcorn. If you can't stand the strain, you invite them over at beddy-bye time, and all you need is the popcorn and, of course, ear plugs for yourself.

"It's great," Pam explained. "If they are really young, they just fall asleep, especially those who suck their thumbs or bring their teddy bears."

"But, Pam," I said, "I'm not sure it is a healthy past time. These kids who aren't getting enough sleep are the future of this country — the brains and the brawn. What if they grow up incurable insomniacs? What if they go to college and still have slumber parties?"

"They do. Then they're called sleep-ins. Don't you remember? Of course, adult slumber parties have different names."

"Don't tell me," I pleaded.

Flying High

All mothers should go away by themselves for at least a week.

Whereas my husband's suitcase has stickers from London and Lisbon and prestigious airline tags, my suitcase has to be dusted off, divested of my grandmother's wedding dress and aired out — all before I can go.

But go I did — for a week. I flew to visit a dear friend in Cleveland. It was so long since I'd traveled alone we had to sew my return ticket in the hem of my raincoat.

It's a levitating experience, a real high. No meals to plan or cook, no dishes, no wondering where the kids are and if they will miss that "quality time" I'm meant to give them when I'm with them.

But coming home can be a cultural-domestic shock. I had left a list of instructions pinned on the refrigerator. I shouldn't have bothered. If it had been their final exams, they all would have failed.

Someone had vacuumed, but no one has dusted. But somebody had written in dust on a table, "Welcome home, Mom."

Dishes were done. But six iced tea glass that had been stacked were stuck together, forever. A plastic pitcher and some plastic spoons had melted in the dishwasher. Someone had done laundry and it was folded on top of the refrigerator. When I put it away, I inquired why there was no underwear — "for one week!"

"Well, Mom, we were too busy to worry about little things, but we didn't catch cold."

Someone had fed the cats. But the cats had eaten two of my plants.

Then the children gave me the good news, which should always be given first, by the way.

• Mike pitched a no-run, no-hit game.

• Daddy cleaned out his old Navy footlocker.
• We learned to make quiche.
• And we didn't have to make a bed because no one came over.

The list went on. I sighed the sigh of universal motherhood and said, "Wait, I wonder if I have time to fly away again?"

Cleveland may not be Bermuda, then neither is home. And home won't ever be a week in Cleveland with a dear friend.

New Mothers, There is Life Beyond the Mall

Ceci has mallmania. She goes to a mall every day.

"You have to understand," she tells me, "it's a way to get out with the baby even in bad weather. I put her in the stroller, she loves it. Sometimes I don't buy anything."

But I still worry that after the baby is in college, Ceci will be so addicted that she'll still go to the mall everyday just to shop, like my friend Hortense.

(Hortense is 55. She goes "mall-dogging" every day and does buy something. In fact, Geraldo had a show on the Hortenses of the world who can't stop shopping.)

"No," says Ceci, "you have to understand, there is a big difference between shopping and buying. Buyers are obsessive compulsives, I'm just taking my baby for a walk, for goodness sakes."

I still think Ceci has a problem. I told her to read a recent article by Sheila Anne Feeney in the New York *Daily News*. Feeney said that catalog-shopping sales are up because many people don't find comfort in malls. The sources of anxiety range from sales people who snub shoppers who aren't dressed well to real agoraphobia — the abnormal fear of being in public places. The article says 25 percent of the population experiences tension and anxiety in malls.

The article goes on: "Those who do brave the stores sometimes buy unwanted items to alleviate feelings of guilt."

Ceci denies that. She says, "I don't have any feelings of guilt. I just feel sorry for people who don't have a mall within two miles of their home to browse in."

I think malls are for people who don't mind smelling a mixture of new polyester, old popcorn, fresh chocolate chip cookies and strong perfume. They are for people who can stand the overtones of babies screaming for another balloon.

Malls are for people who like to charge things, but don't like to stay home with their pile of unpaid bills.

Malls on Saturday are for twittering, trysting 14-year-olds who aren't allowed to date; for young mothers whose babies are teething; and for bored fathers who can't say, "No, I don't want to go to the mall today. There's a game." The biggest mall anxiety comes from trying to find a parking place and wondering where the bathrooms are.

I suggested to Ceci that she try another route for strolling to keep the baby from thinking that life is just one big chain of glass store fronts, fig trees, fountains and bright lights — that somewhere out there are green slopes, sea gulls and beaches.

"You don't understand. What did you do when you had a new baby and felt trapped?" she asks.

Well, I put on big-band records and danced around the house with baby in my arms, or I went to see another friend who felt trapped with her baby and we sat around and griped about our husbands while the babies exchanged cold germs and grabbed each other's hair. It was very therapeutic.

"See, there you are. You were grounded and miserable," Ceci says.

Not really, I loved it. There were no malls. There were things called corner grocery stores and soda fountains.

Chapter 6

A *Thorn* in my *Side* and *Dust* on the *Furniture*

Blooming Gardener a Thorn in Her Side

There are the compulsive golfer, the compulsive tennis player and the compulsive gardener, and they all come out of the woodwork about this time of year.

I married the "garden variety."

If you are married to a compulsive gardener, I don't have to tell you how rewarding this hobby can be, but it also can cause some marital discord.

Take 6 o'clock Saturday morning. I awakened to the noise of a lawn mower.

It was him — he was mowing the lawn.

He came in smiling, sweating, puffing and chortling. "I got 'em this time."

"But you just mowed yesterday. What did you get other than a lot of flack from the neighbors?" I asked.

"I got all those maple seeds that had fallen during the night."

Like a little kid ordering from a mail order house, he leafs and looks through thousands of seed catalogues in the fall. After he has ordered, in come the seeds and then the bulbs. Things that come in lumpy-bumpy packages.

Anything that will grow and isn't tied down he'll plant and pet. It's weird to give someone you love topsoil for his birthday and fertilizer for Christmas, but I did.

Where once we had books and literary magazines, we now have row after row of seed catalogues and jars of insecticide. He has more bottles of weed-goodbye than I have of perfume.

Where once we talked over decisions about our jobs or whether to let the kids have a slumber party, we now have to discuss the germinating time of eggplants.

Where once we discussed where we were going on vacation, we now have to discuss if we have enough lady bugs to kill the aphids.

Where once we displayed tennis trophies, we now have a collection of the latest in oscillating sprinklers with time cutoffs.

Recently, I vacuumed under a bureau and I vacuumed up and away, by mistake, of course, a tray of infant tuberous begonias that were quietly waiting to be put out.

Instead of smelling like men's aftershave, he has a slight aroma of mulch.

When I said to him last night, "Dear, you've been so busy gardening that you didn't notice that I got a new haircut," he jumped up from his chair and said, "Oh, that reminds me, I've got to run out and prune Helen Traubel. ..."

That's a rose by any other name.

Chipped Edges, Fruit Flies
Mean More than Being 'In'

"My kitchen is dead," I told him.

"What?"

"Just what I said, our kitchen is dead. I just finished a magazine article about beautiful kitchens, and suddenly my kitchen and I have an inferiority complex," I said.

"But it cooks so well," he adds, "and it has a dishwasher, a garbage disposal, a mix-master, a blender, a refrigerator, stove and even an electric can opener. Your kitchen and you are spoiled, I think. What more do you want?"

"You don't understand. It's not our appliances, it's just that the kitchen doesn't have that 'au natural' look, that 'in' look, that 'careless-abandon-decorator look.'

"Like here's this kitchen" — I opened the magazine and showed him — "the green refrigerator matches the stove, the tea kettle and the measuring cups.

"And in our kitchen the only things that match are the kids' fingerprints on all the cabinet doors.

"And here's another. All the pans are copper and they are hanging from the wall. Isn't that cute?"

"But you wouldn't hang our pots up," he says. "They have dirty bottoms."

"... And look at these kitchens, they have beautiful bowls of fruit in wicker baskets on the counters. And here's a pewter bowl with shiny green peppers, avocados, carrots and artichokes on the cutting board top. The color scheme even matches her pots and pans."

"Listen to me, you tried that fresh fruit thing in a kitchen basket last year for effect, remember? And we had fruit flies in the house all winter. Then remember the green pepper that had a worm hole in it, and the worm crawled into the apples ..." he tells me.

"Wait, here's a kitchen where the floral wallpaper matches the floral design on her ceramic canisters. ..." and I showed him.

"Floral wallpaper would make our kitchen look even smaller than it is. Don't you realize those pictures are mocked up for the magazine? Our kitchen isn't dead; their kitchens are dead.

"And look, there are no dirty dishes on the sink or half-opened boxes of cereal. No one really lives there," he said. "Besides, I remember when the kids gave you those canisters. And here's the chipped one. You chipped it right before you got your first pair of glasses. You can't give those away," he said.

"OK, you win, you're making me cry. We'll keep the same, old canisters, the same, old children and our same, old kitchen," I said, as I ran my finger lovingly over the chipped edge of the same, old canister.

Mower Power to You

Now don't get mad at me when I say I love lawn mowers. Let me count the ways. Let me explain anyway. And don't send me your tired and broken-down lawn mowers.

Sunday was a lovely, sunny, May day. Flowers were blooming, tra la, la, la, and the time of the singing of the birds had come, when I heard the hum of my neighbor's lawn mowers. Yes, over those birds, of course. I love that noise. Because it means spring has sprung, and summer is here.

And with the lawn mowers comes the whiff of newly mown grass, good for a couple of sneezes and lots of memories of childhood grass stains and fresh grass-cutting smells.

What's that you say? You think I'm crazy, and you hate your lawn mower.

That's just why you and your lawn mower get into trouble. Hating your lawn mower is like hating the sides of your crib when you are 9-months-old. Stupid. You must feed a lawn mower and pet it. In order to have a meaningful relationship with your lawn mower, you must love it.

Come on, lawn mower haters — be glad that you have a lawn to mow. City people have to jog on sidewalks to exercise, but you can mow. People in El Paso, Texas, have to use artificial grass in their back yards and around their swimming pools.

Of course, the men in my family have to do the lawn mowing, but that's not because I am woman. It's because I am the kiss of death to all things mechanical. But yesterday I wanted to help out, and, after all, it was spring. So I pulled on that dumb rope thing. Until I heard a male voice yell, "Did you give it some gas or maybe it's out of oil."

I poured in the oil and pulled again that dumb little rope thing and tried to pretend I was starting a boat when he yelled, "Try the choke."

Choke him or the lawn mower? I followed his directions.

Nothing. "It's all yours, dear," I yelled.

So I sat on the porch and watched while he mowed. And I thought about how much I loved lawn mowers and summer. I'll just wait it out. They can put a man on the moon, so surely they can find a grass that just grows one inch high.

Just Don't Press Her on This One Issue

Once upon a midday dreary:
I waited for the washing machine repair man who never came by;
I found a rip in a brand new dress;
A man had just yelled at me because I didn't make a right hand turn in the "right hand turn lane";
I lost a story I had written.
It was a bummer.

Then I saw them — 12 men's handkerchiefs to iron. I said aloud, "No, no, never, never again. He must learn to blow his nose on Kleenex." I decided not to iron them.

Anyway, that's when it hit me. I hadn't ironed in six months because everything is polyester or wash and wear, and wrinkly cotton is "in."

I decided to give my iron away. That's real liberation.

But as I looked at it, I had a pang of nostalgia. Should I have a going-away ceremony, some witnesses, a party?

After all, that iron had stuck with me many years. The times I've sworn at it for scorching blouses, taking off buttons — all those things irons do when you aren't looking.

I called a daughter. "I'm going to throw away my iron. …"

"Mom, you should have done that five years ago."

I called my best friend. "I'm going to give my iron away, do. …?"

"Don't give it away. Hang it on the wall as an artifact from the middle 1900s," she tells me.

I called my son. "I'm going to give my iron away."

"Mom, I don't care, I always ironed my shirts between the pages of that big encyclopedia anyway."

I called another daughter. "Would you like my nice iron, dear?"

She said, "What's an iron?"

Finally, I called my husband at the office.

"I'm going to throw away my iron."

"Don't do that," he yells. "We may need it. Synthetic clothing may go out of style."

"Then I will, too," I yell back.

"You will what?"

"Go out of style. You see, if ironing comes back in, I will have forgotten how," I explain.

"Wait," he says, "before you throw it away, could you iron that linen shirt? I want to wear it to. ..."

"The iron, dear, is in the garbage can, but I saved the long cord. ..."

Spring is Here: Get Out a Hoe

I don't need daffodils to tell me spring has arrived. I have the man of the house.

He first asks for his 1930 floppy-brimmed, yellow-with-age tennis hat. Then he spends a lot of time looking over the 9 x 9-foot patch of ground we call a garden, as it if were The Ponderosa.

He leans on a pitchfork and chews a piece of straw. (I wonder where he got it?) Clearly a bad case of spring fever. Then he asks, "Has anyone seen my rotary tiller? And where are my hoe and rake?"

Naturally, I get everything out. I even waterproof his fishing boots in case he gets tired of digging. But I keep my distance when the spring planting begins. You see, I have such a way with plants that they wilt if I get too close.

I have managed to amass some tips on gardening, though, and here they are:

- Use string to plant evenly, and attach old white handkerchiefs or scraps of white underwear to the string, so no one will trip. (Last year, I tripped on an unmarked string and fell in the herb garden, mixing up the oregano seeds with the catnip.)
- No matter how bad a gardener your husband is, be thankful. Remember, he could be out on the golf course on weekends instead of being with you in two feet of mud. Let him plant his favorite crops — even parsnips.
- Make sure you can use what you grow. Last year we planted rutabagas, kale and hot peppers. Later, I had to go up and down the street with a loaded wheelbarrow trying to give the stuff away.
- Kids are good weeders, but don't expect an unlimited supply of free labor. And today's young workers are militant. You may have to agree to a list of non-negotiable demands before the first weed is pulled.

Spring Cleaning is So Demeaning

I just can't stand spring house cleaning, and it just can't stand me.

But I'm compelled to pretend to do it so that I'll be socially acceptable in my neighborhood and peer group.

But does every housewife do it? Do women's lib members do it? Do birds do it? (Yes, from an ornithologist friend — some birds are monomaniacs about keeping their nests clean). Leave it for the birds, I say. And I'll bet educated fleas don't do it.

So I do it every spring. In the neighborhood I used to live in, spring house cleaning was a tribal rite. My next door neighbor, Arabella White, put on a head scarf, a cotton dress, tennis shoes and stayed in her house for three days doing it.

But what I'm getting at is what do they really do? Do they cheat like I do? I used to see her on her hands and knees scrubbing her front porch as soon as spring stuck.

Then she opened all the windows in her house and placed pillows on the sills. Then she'd hang out all her blankets and rugs on her clothes line. I never had enough blankets to make a showing. She had 11 blankets, but just one child.

Then all day long I could see her flitting from window to window reaching high, bending low, dusting with a feather duster. Or maybe she was dancing, I dunno. Oh, yes, she put out her indoor plants for an airing, and she'd run the vacuum for three days straight, and the waxer!

So the first spring there, I did it, too. I wanted to belong.

I hung out my four throw rugs on the tree limbs, I didn't have a clothes line yet. I kept them out there for four weeks so that all the neighbors could see them, and know that I was doing my spring cleaning.

Also, I was hoping that the rain would wash them or that lightning might strike them. I turned on the TV loudly, so that the people next door couldn't hear that I didn't have on the vacuum. I put out my four cacti and my two venus fly traps. They died.

I hung out all four of my blankets on the lilac bush out back, and the neighborhood kids played Indian tepee under them for days.

Then I paid one of the kids to wash my front porch at night so they wouldn't see I didn't do it myself. I kept the windows open for three days until a windstorm blew in a bunch of my clean neighbor's new topsoil.

But I was doing it.

You see, I just don't think spring house cleaning is something you should rush into. I don't think it should be done in a hurry. I like my way better. I clean lightly, about twice a week, and I don't even have to wear a head scarf. I just put on my dark glasses and fake eyelashes and sweep it all out.

If you need violent exercise, I say go to the YMCA.

Some say cleanliness is next to godliness, but I think too much cleanliness is telling your husband when he comes home at night that you're too tired to fool around with him!

I saw Arabella's husband the other day in the supermarket buying a new detergent, and I asked him what it's like to come home to a fresh house now that it's spring. He shrugged and said, "Fresh house ... stale wife."

But it's spring now, and I'm opening all the windows so I can smell nice, clean air from my old neighborhood. I can't wash the front porch, because I had it taken off several months ago.

Chapter 7

Spaghetti Straps and Stretch Marks

Buying a New Bathing Suit Calls for a Stiff Upper Lip, Tunnel Vision

Time to get that flabby body back into the bathing suit, gals.
You have these choices:

- You can buy your bathing suit early before you get to the beach or pool, thereby exposing your out-of-shape body to scrutiny in the store's three-way mirror. And remember, that mirror on the left shows your double chin.
- Or you can get your suit on sale toward the end of summer, exposing yourself to unadmiring glances in your old bathing suit that was worn 15 pounds ago.
- Or get the suit now, when you have some tan. And remember there's a chance you may lose some weight during try-on time, while you're squeezing into suits in the fitting room

I decided on the last gambit.

I tried to lock the salesgirl out of the dressing room while I tried on at least 22 bathing suits. She managed to peek in just once. Took a disdainful look and said, "Maybe a cute bathing cap would help?"

Although the one piece suit was suited to my age, some of the two-piece suits can be mixed 'n' matched, just in case you are shaped like a bowling pin or a fat-breasted robin.

I mean, if you take a size 32 bikini top, but a size 40 bikini pants, you can pull a switcheroo. In fact, I've often wondered what the store does at the end of the summer when they probably have all those leftover voluminous and midget-sized bikini pants.

I tried on the way-out suit that looked too scanty for a Barbie doll to take on her honeymoon. It was surely not to swim in, nor to sun in — not even to sleep in. And not to be immersed in water deeper than a bread box. But it was to just pretend in — that for two seconds I was Raquel Welch.

The bathing suit was black, and the G-string bottom was held to the "hardly-any-bra" top by a gold chain. There were no sides and hardly any front. ... Then I thought, no, Raquel won't buy that one either. The chain might rust.

Anyway, that's what I told the salesgirl.

So I ended up with a one-piece conservative suit with a pink sailboat on the skirt.

But at least MY suit made a statement. If you have it, flaunt it — a pink sailboat that is.

Watching Weight-Watcher Watch Diet is Ordeal, Too

Watching a weight-watcher watch his diet is quite a spectator sport.

There's been much written by dieters, doctors and just plain eaters on how to diet, or what it's like to diet. But the literary cupboard is bare on what it's like to live with a dieter.

First, a definition: fatophile, a person who is overweight, always dieting, and wants everyone else to diet, too.

You will notice there is a pattern when he starts his diet. First, he talks about food, then helpings, calories, sugar, salt, proteins, water intake and output, sex and the accuracy of the bathroom scales.

Here's my diary:

On the first day of his diet, my true love said to me, "One case of skimmed milk, two loaves of diet bread, four bushels of carrots — and don't plan any parties."

"Yes, dear."

On the second day of his diet, my true love said to me, "Come look, I'm down two pounds. Look at my pants; they are practically falling off."

"Yes, dear."

On the third day of his diet, my true love said to me, "I'm down three pounds, I've just got 32 to go. But I think I will put a little dressing on my lettuce tonight."

"Yes, dear. I'll sprinkle a little lemon juice on it."

On the fourth day of his diet, my true love said to me, "While driving home from work today, I got very hungry, and almost ate the road maps and drank the antifreeze. So I ate the end of my pipe stem, and I gained a pound.

"I tell you I'm starving, starving. Can we have dinner at 4:30 p.m. instead of 7 from now on?" he asked.

"Yes, dear, and we'll have breakfast at 6:30 in the morning."

On the fifth day, sixth day, seventh day, eighth day, ninth day, 10th day and the 11th day, my true love didn't say anything. He was too weak.

On the 12th day of his diet, my true love said to me, "It's the 12th day and I've only lost three pounds. I think I'm inhaling the things that you are cooking. I wish you and the kids could eat somewhere else." "No dear, maybe you ought to eat somewhere else. Like a health camp. Now, there's one in Colorado, and as a matter of fact, there's a new one in Switzerland."

"OK, OK," he said. "Don't be funny, I'm too weak to laugh. I'm going to start counting calories instead of days. Let's see, at 800 calories a day, and in 12 more days ..."

"Yes, dear," I said, as I longed for 13 lords-a-leaping.

Younger than Springtime?
Follow the (Bathing) Suit

Having the winter doldrums? Long for sunny skies and blue waters? I
have a solution — go look for an early bathing suit. It will make you feel
younger than springtime (or older than winter). But it will give you the illu-
sion that summer is really coming.

When you approach the rack of brightly colored suits, don't be intimidated by the salesgirl, put your chin up, your chest out (if you have one) and
your stomach in (and I know you have one).

She will look you up and down and say, "Oh, we're going on a cruise?"
or "A bathing suit? Wonderful you should buy now. They will all be gone
soon," and before you can say, "French Rivieria," you're in a fitting room
with her and 36 bathing suits that she likes.

Here are some hints: If your winter flesh (areas between your bust and
navel; areas between your upper thighs and ankle bones; area between your
clavicle and chin) is very white, pasty or veiny, then wear a colored body
stocking. The first thing that will scare you are those 8-way mirrors in the
fitting room. Don't stand profile; this can be a real mental tragedy, for you
and the suit.

Don't let the saleslady in the room with you, because she's apt to find out
you are trying on parts from two suits, like the bottom from a size 42 suit,
and the top from a size 32. She says things like, "Don't worry, you'll lose
some of that before summer." (How could she know that you've been trying
to lose "that" for 15 summers.) Or she says, "I know, my daughter has big
hips, too. She wears a suit with a skirt." Don't take a good friend with you,
as she will say each one looks great, because she doesn't want her husband

to think you're cute in your new suit. And don't take your teen-age daughter. She'll say too much. And your mother won't do either. Try on suits with the most coverage first, and then keep trying until you get to the kind you want — sexy. ... Let's face it, that's the look you're striving for. (If you're not, don't go near the water.)

And remember I didn't tell you to go on that banana and crackers shape-up-or-slip-out-diet, did I? Or that 20 knee bends or jogging in place for two weeks will help? All you really need is courage and guts in all the right places to buy your preseason suit.

This year, there are suits for everyone. If you have no bust, they have suits with enough foam rubber to keep you from drowning in a tidal wave. There are suits with frothy apron fronts that hang over your midriff, in case you have a purple gall bladder or high hernia scar.

They have suits with sleeves in case you have fat shoulders, or black moles under your arm. The bikinis this year have tops that are as small as Band-Aids, and bottoms that look like a Barbie doll diaper.

I bought my bathing suit at 4:45 p.m. Thursday, and at 7 p.m. I was in it standing in front of him while waiting for dinner — he was reading the paper at the time — and I said, "how do you like it ... ?"

"Lean, you know that," was his simple answer.

So you might try this little poem as you are contemplating your new suit.
"Mirror, mirror on the wall,
Do I have the guts and gall,
Standing here oblong and raw
To wear this bathing suit?"

So You Really Think
It's Fun Being One of the Silent Thin

I'm sick of all these diet-minded people. It was bad enough to go to lunch with three friends, all of whom could only drink or eat cyclamated food or polyunsaturated things.

Now, when I go to lunch with those same three, they count every grain of sugar on their grapefruit and the monosodium glutamate in their peas. They leave the olive in their martinis and eat the parsley stems on their plates!

Just once I'd like a friend to say instead of "No, thank you," when the dessert came by, "Yes, please and I'll take four."

Of course, I will admit there is a certain type, like my neighbor Elisabeth, who weighs 250 pounds before her bath and with her hair cut short. She orders soda crackers for lunch when you take her out, but says she is so hungry by dinner that she nibbles on her cat's Friskies and eats two helpings of everything for dinner, with side dishes of butter, sugar and whipped cream.

I want to talk about women who are thin and skinny, or just bony, for that matter. Do you know what it's like to grow up in a fat family and be thin? It can leave a lasting imprint on you.

Do you know what it's like to go to a girls' school and always have to play the male lead in the annual play because you are the tallest and the thinnest girl in the class? I've played Malvolio in "Twelfth Night," Huckleberry Finn in "Huckleberry Finn" and Dracula and his girl friends in "Dracula."

From 10- to 12-years-old, I slept on my back so I wouldn't mash my chest. When I was 11, I tied my brother's soccer shin guards on my hips to pad them. When I had my Girl Scout picture taken, I put marshmallows in my mouth to give me fat cheeks.

Do you know what it's like to be 14 and female and have a tailor tell you that if he takes the back seam in on your band uniform the back pockets will meet?

And when you finally get to age 16 and the saleslady says to you, "You can wear it, dearie, you're so thin." If I've heard that once, I'd heard it 48 times, and 48 skirts have slipped off my skinny hips.

Then there is the salesman who said, "Oh, you are so nice and thin, you ought to model," but he told me to go to the boys' department for my sweaters.

Wherever you go, people tell you about their diets. What a bore, if you are thin. At a cocktail party recently, a man with a huge stomach told me about the year he stood on his head twice a day to redistribute his weight. His ankles were skinny.

My fat friend Dora said she lost 20 pounds on a boiled bananas-in-rice-gruel diet, but then she had indigestion for six months, too.

Ginny up the street has invented a calorie Geiger counter that she used on her dinner plate to count the calories, because she gained four pounds during Lent.

I think fat people are jollier and cuter. Really, when your skin is stretched tightly over your body, it's harder to relax.

I say there is a bunch of silent majority thin people. There is no special counter for them in the grocery shop or the dress shop. All they really inherit is a seat on the crowded subway or looks of envy from their overweight friends.

Why, my mother once made my bed while I was still in it. But time changes all things. I finally found out how to gain weight: "Drink two beers before each meal with"… whoops, there I go giving you another diet.

The Bathing Suit Tryouts
or The Skinny on New Suits

I'm trying to stay calm. After all, it will only be for four days, maybe only for four hours a day. And I don't mean having to listen to hard rock music in a room with no exit. No, it's being on a beach in a bathing suit this time of year. It's the idea of wearing a bathing suit when you're past the water ski-ing years. It's like trying to encase residue, you know, that extra "something" we're all carrying around from Thanksgiving and Christmas eat-a-thons, into one piece of brief material. It's having to wear it in front of people I don't know — or worse, do know. Either way, it's a bad scene.

A friend and I are contemplating flying on a weekend package to a beach in the Bahamas. And the bad part is that at my age I do not go on a watercress diet before vacationing. Nor do I want to disrupt the swimsuit departments at local stores with my bare white legs showing blue streaks, which I call veins. Then there are lumps and bumps from years of gnashing my shins on the dishwasher door when it's open. And let's not forget all the brown spots on the legs, which may be freckles or, more likely, scars from where I've cut myself shaving over the years. (Here's a tip to avoid a demeaning trip to the department store. Avoid taking your 5-year-old grandchild into the dressing room with you, because the quite-inventive one may say, "Nana, we can play dot-to-dot with my magic marker between those brown spots on your legs.")

Don't deny this, women. Bathing suit tryouts are trauma and drama in cold, cold weather. For any woman over 40, trying on suits is like squeezing toothpaste back into the tube.

There are tricks you can initiate, like wearing an oversized beige leotard that covers your bosoms when pulled up. Or you can take a few of the bulbs out of the track lighting in your new brightly lit bathroom. But you can't do that in front of a three-way mirror at the local department store.

Here's the skinny on this season's helpful instructions to make customers feel more able to make a decision. Manufacturers have "hang tickets" that are on the better suits with a list of options for the imperfect figure — the bust enhancer, the hip minimizer, the boob reducers or, even, the waist reducer. One bathing suit I loved was tagged the full-motion athletic fit, for I guess, a Jane Fonda body — it was an "all-in-one suit." Then there are the more descriptive notes, like "the bust increaser with waist decreaser and minimalist hip design." Soon, it just becomes confusing, and you start to sweat. Sweating is not an option, however. But even with these new fangled tags, it is still hard to find a suit that is a 10 on top and a 12 on the bottom.

It is also extremely intimidating when the trim salesperson asks you, "What size are you, hon?" There should be a law against that question. And don't let the salesperson go into or near your dressing room. It should be like a confessional — private, just between you and the mirror. Also, do not go into one of those big fitting rooms where all the women try on clothes together. Believe me, it is not like being at Camp Winnapawookie when you were 9.

I guess the most important thing to remember is: Don't give up. A very fat man, wet or dry, in a string bikini will look a lot worse than you, and make you feel like Cindy Crawford. Oh yes, did I tell you, "pads" for the bra-top bathing suits are for sale, usually hanging nearby, and they don't float away when a big wave hits you.

Chapter 8

Marital Mess

For Couples, Never a 'Love' Game

A tennis-playing friend of mine said to me recently, "All the people my wife and I play tennis with get a divorce."

Now, I've been thinking about Don's statement. It bears pondering. I called the National Association of Tennis Buffs, the U.S. Mixed Doubles Temperance Society and the National Association of Partners Without Marriages trying to find statistics.

"It's too soon to know," one spokesman said. "Family tennis has only been a big craze in the past five years. Call us later."

I know what Don means. I remember when my husband and I used to be tennis partners. It was no "love" game, I'll tell you. When we changed sides with our opponents, he'd whisper through clenched teeth, "Why in the devil did you take that last shot at the net? You should have dropped back. Can't you run backwards?"

And then there was the summer after he'd taken lessons and he started to wear wristbands and hog my side of the court. He'd yell at me when I was about to apply my overhead slam, "It's mine, all mine."

We'd lose the point and the match, too, and we wouldn't speak for days.

I remember one match we played (it was right after I'd bought a darling see-through tennis dress). He came up to me between sets and told me, "Pin your hair back, you can't even see the ball. ... And do you have to lean over so much?"

We even tried mix 'n' match doubles. You know, that's where you split up husband and wife teams. My husband calls it Picnic Tennis, because some 2-year-old wanders out on the court while furious play is on and screams, "Mommy, mommy, potty, potty."

Or someone's dog lopes onto the court and fetches all the bouncing balls.

And, worse still, an irate non-tennis playing wife pulls up in the station wagon with three crying kids and yells, "Fred, Fred, come quick. The washing machine is overflowing."

So, like the joint checking account, the together tennis games came to an end. We finally knew that if we wanted to play together, we'd better play separately.

Don says, "We've quit playing together, too. Couples who play doubles ask for troubles. Now, you take hand gliding ..."

I Pronounce You Two Cat and Owl

I finally went to one. One of the "new weddings."

First they were called hippie weddings, then counterculture weddings, then alternative weddings, and now they are called contemporary weddings or personal weddings. (Meaning that the ceremony is written by the bride and groom, but performed by a minister.)

So it's June and it's time for weddings and I think it's time for some changes in the traditional weddings.

I had so much fun. I wore what I wear to market, but we could have gone dressed in clown costumes. No one cared.

The wedding took place on top of a small footbridge overlooking a babbling brook and a babbling congregation.

We stood in a circle around the bridge. The groom stood on the bridge. The minister stood on a rock in the water.

I went with a friend, May, who is conservative. Taking May was a mistake. I'm still black and blue from being nudged in the ribs. "Can you believe that?" she'd say every time wedding rites took a new turn.

The groom wore blue jeans and his hair was so long I never saw his shirt. The bride wore a dress she had made from cotton sacking and coronet of fresh (but fading rapidly) daisies in her hair.

My husband wouldn't go because the style of the invitation scared him off. It said, "The owl and the pussycat went to sea in a beautiful pea green boat. They took some honey and plenty of money tied up in a five pound note," and so forth.

Well, at the wedding I didn't see an owl or a pussycat or a boat, but I got the picture that they were going to dance by the light of the moon.

The bride and groom read some poems and sang a song and wind whistled through the trees and my friend May whistled through her teeth.

The background music was rendered by two guitarists and a cow who made an unscheduled appearance.

The maid of honor was barefoot, and the best man had poison ivy. He had to wear Bermuda shorts and calamine lotion on his itchy legs.

Afterward, we drank homemade dandelion wine and ate cheese and played with a goat who had joined the crowd.

May said, "I don't even consider them married."

"May, the minister said they were."

"Yeah, that's because he's on their side."

"Amen," I said.

But hold onto your church seats, because just last week we got invited to another wedding. The invitation read, "A loaf of bread and a jug of wine. And thou."

(I later heard they had a picnic reception with beer and potato chips.)

We didn't go to that one. But my husband has promised he'll go to one if the invitation reads, "Rub-a-dub-dub, three men in a tub" and so forth.

Appliances Can Put a
Marriage Through the Wringer

I guess it happens to lots of couples who go shopping together for a major household item: confrontation, argument and fractious behavior. Oh, please tell me we aren't unusual. (And you out there contemplating marriage, try shopping for a washing machine together before you tie the knot.)

For weeks, we had been comparison-shopping, watching the ads and cutting them out. Our washing machine was starting to spit, burp and cough. Obviously, it was on its last leg, or bearing.

So we took a few evenings to find a bargain. I took my husband with me, because somewhere it says that marriage is 50/50 and because I am supposedly liberated and he is supposedly subjugated. At least, it says in my new handbook, "The average husband is now helping with the household chores."

I mean, he has done a few loads of wash for me. But prior to a case of flu I had in 1979, he didn't know how to turn the machine on. He does know where the kitchen is and has taken a few dishes to the sink. But now it is 1982, and we are supposed to be a team.

Never again. From now on, I will paddle my own canoe. It will be just me and the salesman. Teamwork is screamwork.

The washer he saw first was a bare-bones model in white.

"Look at this bargain. It has everything you'd ever want on it, and it is only $289," he cried out.

"But it doesn't have a built-in filter, all those cycles and three water levels for energy saving," I said.

Then he spied the scratch and dent department.

"Look at these! We can get a real bargain here," he said, caressing a machine with two huge dents on either side. Suddenly, our disagreement became a shouting match, and I wondered which one of us might end up in the scratch and dent department.

He started to bargain with me. "I will do the washing for you if you'll just stay under $200," he pleaded.

"Look at this one," I screamed. "It has five speeds, heavy-duty super-surgilator agitator with an overhead cam engine and four-wheel drive. ..."

"That's a car, you dummy," he yelled. "Besides, does that expensive machine hang out the clothes for you, turn on the oven or fold the laundry?"

"You've blown your mind," I told him and the salesman, who had already mumbled something about re-enlisting in the Marines.

Then I saw a washer that cost more than $500 but came with a lifetime guarantee. It was avocado green, my favorite color, and it did everything.

"Look, I don't like pea-soup green, you know that. And I will bet that for all that money it's not noiseless," snorted my husband.

Well, to make a short story shorter, I went to the car and pouted. Ten minutes later, he appeared carrying a huge carton. A portable TV.

"You've said you always wanted one for the bedroom. Well, here it is."

"But the washing machine. ..."

"It can wait. It's not dead yet. We gave the salesman such a bad time, I thought we should buy something."

"Can that TV turn on the oven, and is it noiseless?" I asked so sweetly.

For a Blissful, Long Marriage, Forget the Car

Recently, a young soon-to-be-married friend asked me, "You've been married a long time; what's your secret to continued success? What have been the worst times in your marriage?"

Well, I had to ponder the questions a long time. One false answer and I might destroy her pink cloud and her trip down the aisle.

These are the days of self-help books and me-tooism and myriads of do's and don'ts about how to stay married or have a lasting relationship. But professionals tell us that the major problems seem to be sex, money, in-laws and lack of communication. In that approximate order.

Well, not so in our marriage. The best advice I gave her was, "Stay out of cars."

You see, romantically speaking, when you start out a relationship the car is a great place to do everything — well, everything within reason. The car's usually where the action is, right?

But now, years later, I look at the car as sort of a devil's advocate. A people's court, a battleground and a war zone.

Sure, I realize America's great love affair with the car. But a car is still a small, confining space for six people or just two, and you are in it almost half your life.

The car is where we've had most of our major arguments. The car is like a battleground for lots of us. We can seal ourselves off by closing the doors and then scream at one another.

It may start six months after you are married, when he goes through his first red light and gets a ticket while insisting it was only yellow. That's good for at least an hour's argument, and will be brought up months later when he makes a left-hand turn from a right-hand lane.

Then when the kids come along, it really gets worse in the car.

In-car trouble makers:

"Did you bring her pacifier?"

"No, I couldn't find it."

"Then she won't go to sleep the whole trip.."

"She shouldn't have a pacifier now, anyway. She's too old; she's 10."

Or "Don't tailgate; the baby has gone to sleep on my arm and I can't get the seat belt fastened."

"I'm not tailgating. Go to sleep. Leave the driving to me."

Or you're 800 miles from home and she says, "Did you pay for the gas and electric before we left home?"

"No, I forgot."

Then later when the kids are older:

"Mom, I can't eat onions. ... Mom, where are the french fries? ... I just spilled catsup on the car seat, Dad. ... I've begged you before, Herbert, can't we take the time to go in and place our orders?"

Or "Did I tell you I let him have your car until midnight?"

"No. That's terrible. When he asked me I said, 'No.' You let him do anything. ..."

Or, "You told me you'd be here by 7:30 and I've been waiting for you in this car since 8:15. Where in the hell have you been?"

"I saw a dress I liked and. ..."

Or you are heading into the Holland Tunnel. "I don't think the brake lights are working. ... They weren't this morning."

Or "Will you ever learn to fold a road map? Get it out of my face, please. I can't see the road."

Or you're coming home from a party. "Wow, did you see the girl in the tight silk dress? She had beautiful legs."

Widow's Weeds Are an Uncomfortable Fit

Last month, I pretended to be a widow.

In the past year, my sister's husband died, my aunt's husband died and three of my best friends' husbands died. I received shock wave after shock wave, and I didn't do too well. I am getting to that age where people die. I am over 50. And the men are going first.

I tried to help my friends, but found I don't know a lot about widowhood. Oh, I'd read the books. The different stages of grief: the anger, the fear, the why me syndrome, the martyr complex, the depressions, the anxiety and, finally, the loneliness.

But what is it really like to suddenly be a widow?

I think middle-aged couples should talk about death when they draw closer to it. I think we should prepare for it, not just emotionally, but also on a business basis. Death is certainly not just the flip side of life; it's part of the life process.

Some of you may think what I'm going to tell you now is weird. But for me, it was an experiment in sharing experiences.

My husband went to California for two weeks, and I was completely alone. I decided to imagine he wasn't coming back. I hadn't been alone in several years, so I decided to see how weak or strong I was. Would I be able to get used to being alone? Had I been too dependent?

Yes, to both questions. I found out I was both weak and strong in areas I didn't know existed.

A few friends called the first night. "Come on over for dinner while he's gone," they said. But they never stipulated when.

The first evening, at the time the two of us usually sit down and have a drink in front of the evening news while dinner is cooking, I sat down with the drink and the news. But I found I don't like drinking alone. And I found there was no one to turn to and say after a news bulletin, "Can you believe that?"

I decided I'd cook a real meal, not heat a frozen one. I made a small salad, and I was going to heat a roll. But it seemed silly to heat the oven for one roll. So I ate it cold.

Should I eat in front of the TV? No, bad habit. So I set a nice place at the table, but there was nothing to look at. I was very lonely. And this was only the first night he was gone.

I took my plate and went into the den and turned the TV back on wishing I had just opened a can on tuna.

Then what would I do after dinner? A little weeding? I went outside, but the garden made me feel lonelier, because this, too, was a shared interest.

Just a Normal Pair of Paranormals

One of the nicest things about being married a long time is that you can learn to read one another's minds, or, as I call it, playing "brain bounce" or "having extramarital telepathy."

Now this is not a lovey-dovey or sex-oriented game to keep your relationship stimulated, but it does keep your mind in high gear.

It's a cerebral game for those who have been married two years to 35 years. And you don't need a computer or a batter to play it. People who have lived together for a long time are like chirping birds: They learn to communicate if they are sharing the same nest. Right?

I didn't realize how well we played it until we were coming home the other day from another city, and we had been in the car together for five hours. Here are some examples of our brain bounce with "speakease."

- Out of the clear blue, I say to him, "I like it, I really do, it's distinguishing. ..."

  And he says, "So do I, but I never would have thought. ..."

  We were talking about a friend's new beard we'd seen two days ago. Though his name was never mentioned, we knew exactly who we were talking about.

- We were driving along and he is telling me about something that happened at his office. In the middle of it, I say, "The eggplant. ..."

  And he says, "I just never liked you in that yellow dress."

  Well, what that meant was that we had just passed a church which reminded him of a church where I had worn a new yellow dress on which I had later spilled eggplant parmigiana.

- Or the other night, as we are looking at a woman on television describing a cleaner for false teeth.

And he says "Zimmie. ..."

Then I said, "Yeah. But Zimmie ... prettier."

Zimmie is my cousin who looked like the girl in the commercial.

Brain bounce is a little like football. You shouldn't lose cadence. You try not to lose the ball. You can intercept, but if you do, the game must run smoothly.

Happiness is never having to finish a sentence with someone you love. But I must warn you, brain bounce can backfire.

We were flying into Cleveland last year. And I said, "The curling rod..."

And he said, "Yeah, I like your hair that way ... those curls ..." He smiled and went on talking to the man next to him.

I interrupted him two flashing "fasten-your-seat-belt" signs later, and said, "No, you don't understand. I think I left the curling rod on in our bathroom."

He didn't speak to me for the rest of the trip. However, it turned out I hadn't left it on.

So it's a pretty, but very cold, blue-skied day today as I write this, and I called him at his office. I said, "It's a beautiful day ..."

And he said, "Let's ..."

And I said, "OK."

Now, that's marital telepathy and we're going hiking in our favorite woods if I can just find my old boots.

Women Can Be Grateful
Without Having to Grovel

It was over at Hope's borrowing an onion when I heard her say to her husband, who had just come home from work, "Oh, honey, I'm so sorry. Dinner is not done yet. Why don't you just sit there and read? It's going to be late. I was kept late typing another proposal at the office and the crock pot broke down and I had to take the kids to practice. I'm so sorry."

So I asked her later, "Hope, why didn't you ask him to help you fix the dinner?"

She looked at me like I'd gone to the moon. "He doesn't know how to cook. And besides," and she lowered her voice, "I get tired of asking."

I thought about this all evening. And I realized that since I went to work many years ago, I have been doing pretty much the same thing, turning the grateful wife into the groveling wife.

I have, indeed, been playing "thank you, thank you."

For instance, when he sometimes would cook on Sundays, I praised him to the skies: "The roast was great, the potatoes were super and your tomatoes were sliced just right. ... Thank you, thank you."

When the children were small and he changed a diaper or bathed somebody, I said, "Thank you, thank you, thank you."

My husband has retired now, and he is helping more, which is great. But I am still doing it. The other day, he did the laundry for the first time, and I lauded him, "Oh, thank you, thank you."

He is doing the vacuuming once a week, and I am saying, "Thank you, thank you." For every household chore he is doing, he is receiving a standing ovation.

Now, don't get me wrong.

"Thank you" is a beautiful phrase. But there are many women like Hope and me out there who, by habit and training, have been abject too long. Dr. Ari Kiev, author of a new book, "How to Keep Love Alive," has a whole chapter on the martyr.

"Self-sacrifice, even though it may appear exemplary on the surface, induces guilt in others, limits their senses of freedom and may destroy a relationship.

"Disguised in the form of greater concern for pleasing your partner than for pleasing yourself, self-sacrifice may backfire.

"Self-imposed martyrdom becomes a problem when people have to decide what to share and how to share. But you have to avoid doing what you don't want half the time and letting your partner do what he or she wants the rest of the time."

The point is, how many times over the years has Hope's husband said, "thank you" for the 365 meals every year she cooked for him or "thank you" for every time his wife bathed their baby?

Times are changing, thank goodness, and no longer does it threaten their masculinity for men to help on the domestic front.

The husband/father is no longer the supreme commander and the wife a second-class seaman. We are, thanks to new thinking, co-pilots.

Do I sound like Betty Friedan? No, I just think it is time that all partners share. Happiness is not having to say "thank you" when he sorts out his own socks.

What Turns You On? Be Honest

What turns you on about the opposite sex? Come on now, be honest.

I mean physically what do you look for, or at, in the opposite sex? I've taken a survey in my block and at my office. The conclusions of which I shall share with you. The older men are either leg men or chest men. The younger men are face men. But one thing they all had in common: they liked women who looked like women.

One old-time chest man said, "The trouble is if she has a size 36-inch top, she has 46-inch thighs." I guess I know how he feels, because my butcher told me to pick a good turkey by the breast size, "fat-breasted turkey means fat thighs and legs."

Of course, there is always one oddball in the group. He said he looked at a woman's teeth first. Had he been a veterinarian or a vampire? No, he liked teeth and thought they were sexy. Just wait until he has to buy some.

Now, the women were more explicit. "I like a man's face to be craggy looking." One said she liked the back of a man's neck, but she couldn't say why. One liked men with "crooked noses but straight bodies," she said.

The younger women said they liked a cross between Sean Connery, Dustin Hoffman and Rock Hudson. One woman added that she looked at a man's hands first — "I like hair on hands, too, and hair on a man's chest is a must."

A national magazine said recently there is more discrimination now against short men than ever before, but in my survey I didn't find this.

They said in a recent survey that among University of Pittsburgh graduates, those 6 feet 2 inches and over are receiving average starting salaries 12.4 percent higher than those under 6 feet and that Americans have always favored tall political candidates.

Now, I think that's mean. Some of my best male friends are short, and I don't know any who would stoop so low as to want to be president.

Short men are good in attic cleanups, lost baseballs in manholes, low tree branches and back seats of cars. Look at Mickey Rooney. He's had six wives, and he's been short forever, right?

In my local survey, I found that height played a very small part, but the weight played a big role. That old saying "beauty is but skin deep" means just that. Don't have too many layers of fat, and it is the first one that counts, the one that's out front — the one that shows!

All Right, Men, Say You're Sorry

I don't think I have to call a psychologist to find out why men can't say they're sorry.

Over the years, I've known scads of men who never said they were sorry.

Men don't say they're sorry because their fathers before them didn't say they were sorry. And I don't believe that line from the wonderful book "Love Story" — "Love means never having to say you're sorry." I think love means saying you are sorry.

Oh, this is mean, but we women are still subservient, used to apologizing and saying we're sorry over the smallest matters.

I bet I say I'm sorry 10 times a day, at work, to my children, even to the clerk who took so long to find my cleaning the other day. He told me he was hung over and I said, "I'm sorry!"

A bunch of us women were sitting around the other day, and I heard a few "sorry" testimonials. First mine:

I remember back in 1956 driving from Texas to Kansas and being late for a funeral, which is something you cannot be late for. I told him to take a certain road — I had the map in my hand — he said I was wrong, and we took the road he suggested.

Needless to say, we got very lost, and if you've ever been lost in Kansas cornfields you know it's not fun. We ended up missing the funeral, which, of course, the deceased didn't mind, but I did. My husband never said he was sorry. I tried to get him to say it during the all-night car trip, but he wouldn't.

Years later — just the other day, in fact — he turned quickly in the kitchen, a place where we don't work well together anyway, and the handle of the wok he was holding hit my elbow. It was unintentional, and I suppose I was lucky he was going to cook something in the first place. I have shown him the bruise again and again — it is turning green now — but he still hasn't said he's sorry. He did say our kitchen is too small and that one of these days he will remodel it.

Then Mollie tells us that in 1983 they were remodeling their house and her husband dropped a two-by-four on her toe, breaking the toe and splintering the wood. And he's yet to say he's sorry. He just said, "Didn't see your foot, hon. You ought to wear heavier shoes. ..."

A 20-year-old sitting next to me tells us that when she and her husband were unpacking their wedding gifts, he dropped a large porcelain vase, an heirloom from her side of the family, and he never said he was sorry. Instead, he speculated, "Why would anyone want a vase that heavy?"

Anne adds that when she went into labor with their first child, she called her husband and told him to come home right away. He didn't, and a neighbor took her to the hospital. Her husband showed up later, right before the baby did. But he never said he was sorry for being late and missing those initial groans, moans and expletives. Anne is still mad.

OK, enough already. I finally called a psychology hotline and got Dr. Sigman Fraud, author of "Women Who Love Men and The Men Who Won't Say They Are Sorry."

"I'm sorry," he said, and I liked that, but then he said, "There is no exact answer, but as a rule, men just don't like defeat or being wrong. ..."

"And women do?" I screeched at him.

"No, it's just that women are accustomed to feeling sorry. It's an inherited behavior pattern, and ..."

I hung up on him, and I'm not a bit sorry.

Chapter 9

Raving
Beauty

A New Wrinkle For Your Face

American women are consumed with the beauty cult. And I'm one of them. We give daily penance, especially to the face. The face is the battleground.

Do this, do that, buy this, buy that. From a $60 bottle of "rip off" cream to pollen from the queen bee, our faces and wallets take a 20th century beating.

Well, I've had it. I may let my face go back to just being a place to hold my eyes, nose and mouth.

Beauty consultants always have something fascinating to say, and they always look beautiful while they say it.

There's one who told me we must get back to basics with cucumbers for astringents, figs for dark circles and garlic for pimples — all of which taste great over a mayonnaise facial base.

Then again, oil from some poor turtle and petroleum jelly will guarantee you a younger face, but you may slip off the pillow case.

Now, I want to share with you the latest wrinkle. A whole book has been written about ironing out your wrinkles with spoons. Good, I thought, because I was tired of using Scotch tape.

All you need is a bunch of spoons. First, you coat your face with oil, preferably sesame or apricot oil. And then you dip a spoon in hot water and iron your wrinkles. But don't let those spoons slip — you'll need your eyes for this exercise.

I've tried it for 30 days now, and I will say I've had no more headaches. However, I do still have my wrinkles, but then I was never any good at ironing. But don't let me kid you, spoon therapy feels great.

I also have three bent spoons. Try to use silver spoons — they retain heat and cold better. If you were born with a silver spoon in your mouth — use that one.

Maybe last week's beauty "hypes" was the most honest. While looking lovely encased in a plastic beauty mask, she took off her rose-colored glasses, looked straight at me and divulged her innermost beauty secrets.

"Stay out of the sun, wind and swimming pools. Get eight to 10 hours of sleep, eat well and above all try not to smile or laugh."

I laughed uncontrollably and told her, "I'd sooner dry up like a tired, old prune."

Poor dear, she frowned — from ear to shining ear.

If It's Peaches, It's Thursday

It was in bed that he found out. I slithered in beside him, a Vaseline coating on my rough heels in my white socks. Toilet paper wrapped round my new hairdo from the beauty parlor, and my flannel nightgown with the two buttons off. Certainly a vision of loveliness and a sex symbol of 1,000 or so married women across this nation who go to the hairdresser's on Thursdays.

As I was drifting into sleep, I heard, "Honey, you smell sort of funny. ... you smell like a fruit stand. What did you do today? Did you go pick peaches with Mary again at that fruit farm?"

"No, guess again. Feel my face?"

He did, "Same nose."

"OK, I confess; I had a fruity facial today at the hairdresser's. I'd never had a facial. That's coconut night cream you smell. They vacuumed and magic-misted my face. Then they put hormones, masks and herbs right down to my neck."

"You're kiddin'," he said. "Did they take off your eyebrows and all those wrinkles?"

"You weren't meant to look at me until morning, I should look much younger by then. I used whipped cream cleanser on my face with turtle oil and lemon-lime skin freshener. I vacuum my rugs. Why shouldn't my face be vacuumed?"

"Look," he said, sitting up by now. "We can get a new rug, but you only have one face. ... I don't think I can go to sleep now," he added.

"Well, I could go to Switzerland and have cell therapy. You know where they inject the serum from the unborn lamb into you and it makes you feel younger."

"I'm OK. Go ahead and go to sleep. ... count sheep," I suggested, as I floated into a dream of dancing through fruit orchards with gamboling lambs.

Orange Home-Dye Job Blows Neighbor's Top

Myra Deckenridge, my neighbor, called the other morning, "Please, can you come over quick? I'm in a jam...I need your help."

Quickly, in my mind, I thought, "Her husband left her a goodbye note (he's always threatening)? Her hippie kid left and didn't leave a goodbye note? Or her 5-year-old ran away with her car?"

"I'll be right there," I said.

I threw on my bathrobe, my good one, which I reserve for emptying the garbage or taking the kids to school in the morning. The one I reserve for state things.

When I got there, I discovered that Myra's head had turned orange.

"I dyed my hair for our anniversary, and it's turned orange," she said between sobs (Myra's hair was naturally gray).

"Can you run to the drugstore for me and get something. ...?"

I ran, in my bathrobe, and then I put Myra's head into the sink, put on those skinny plastic gloves that come with dye kits, and started in.

"Myra, what happened?"

"Well, I was dyeing my hair when the phone rang, and it was Hedda telling me about her trouble with Harry, and I never heard the timer. Also her troubles sounded so much like mine. I wanted to be blonde, now I'm orange. ..." Sob, sob.

"Myra, are you going out tonight for dinner? Will the place be dark?" I questioned.

"No, he's taking me to the bowling alley."

"You can't go. What about that fur hat of yours?"

"I can't wear it, it's spring, remember?"

"What about your red wig?" I asked.

"I can't wear that, either — the crickets ate it last year."

"Look, Myra, you have to know something, this brown may not work, you may come out 'Brorange.'"

She started to cry again.

"Myra, do you have a turban. ...?" I gently asked.

"They are out of style ... and so am I, that's the trouble."

When we finished with her hair, she looked pretty good. Her hair was slightly brorange, with gold roots.

She looked in the mirror.

"Oh, you've done such a good job, what can I do for you?"

"Don't dye your hair ever again, please," I begged.

But I have to explain the reason I was called in on the case. All the neighbors know about the time I dyed my hair green.

I tried an ash blond dye called "shampoo in," and the minute my scalp turned purple, I knew something was happening that wasn't good. I am by nature a dirty blonde.

While I was turning green (my hair, that is), I drove to the nearest hairdresser, wrapped in a towel (my hair, that is).

When I got there, I whispered my trouble and asked if there was a private booth, for the unveiling.

"My dear, the only private booths we have are for electrolysis, hair removal. ..." but as she said it, she peeked under the towel.

"We'll give you over to Mr. Marilyn. He's good on stripping. ..." (Hair, that is.)

Before I could say "strip," I was sitting under the glare of bright lights, with Mr. Marilyn saying, "Stay calm, we can go ahead and strip you, and you'll be back to normal. We see a lot of this."

Needless to say, everyone saw my green hair, and everyone laughed, but I bit my fingernails. But I was never quite normal. Since that day, however, I became the neighborhood authority on dyeing and ringworm on kids.

Another thing, since I am really a blonde, my friends think it's out of the bottle. Actually, the only time I use a whole bottle of anything is when I pour Liquid-Plumr down the bathtub drain.

15 Yards Given for Face-Masking

Remember the day when a teen-ager's room smelled like crayons, pencil lead, tired tennis shoes, gym suits and dirty socks?

Well, call on a teen-ager today, if you have one. I did.

It's different now.

I knocked first, and then went in and smelled what seemed to be a fresh tossed salad and strawberry sundae.

"Whatcha doin'?" I asked.

"I'm making my own cosmetics," she said uneasily, as if I'd caught her making gin in the bathtub. "You can, too, Mom. You could sure use some avocado skin oil on those dry spots."

She has shelves of strawberry facial mask, lemon and orange oils, carrot and cucumber astringents and green apple shampoos.

"It's getting back to earth and basics with natural sources, " she explained to her poor, dumb mother, who used to be content with a jar of cold cream from the 5-and-10-cent store.

"Look, dear, I've put up with a lot of things in these rooms, including gerbils, aquariums, snakes and chemistry sets, but wouldn't it be better to make some of this goo in the kitchen? Those carrot shreds are getting on the carpet."

"Sure, Mom, if you'll promise you'll try my citrus facial mask," she answered.

"OK, although I think it is a little late for me."

I tried it. Here's the recipe:

Citrus Facial Mask: beat one egg, fold into three ounces each of orange juice and lemon juice. Mix well. Apply to face and leave on 20 minutes. Then rinse.

How did I look? Great. My face smelled like a lady's day cocktail hour, but it was a little drawn up, kind of prune-like at the corners.

But one good thing about these new "back to earth" cosmetics. If you don't like them, you can always lick 'em off.

Chapter 10

Grandmother, What Big Memories You Have

Still Waiting for Father's Day

I see a young father swinging his little boy in the park. The sounds of the 3-year-old laughing, his head thrown back in glee, and the sun dappling the scene are a Father's Day hallmark for me. Later, the father and the little boy spread a blanket to have a picnic.

This brings a pang of sadness and intense longing. I never remember my father swinging me, and we had a swing.

But then I never knew my father.

I never knew what he was really like, or if he loved me. Or if I loved him.

No, he didn't die when I was a baby, but his spirit died with the Great Depression when the better part of a whole generation lost its will.

He was a figurehead as nebulous as the future for those of us who were post-Depression children.

Of Quaker parents, he was very self-contained. But then, a lot of fathers of that generation were remote in parenting and domesticity. And that's why I love to see the fathers of today with their nurturing skills and their ability to play Mr. Mom if need be.

I just can't remember my father playing with me.

I do remember while he was waiting for the world to get better, he often played our piano and sang. We weren't exactly the Partridge family.

During my growing-up years, he would sit by the radio, smoking a cigar, looking at the want ads for jobs but never going to see about them.

His spirit was gone, and he started to drink. Many men did.

But I also knew a neighbor who went out in the woods and shot squirrels so his family would have enough to eat. And my mother started supporting us in various ways — teaching in the daytime, making cakes for a cake shop and reading to a wealthy blind lady at night — all to keep us in food and clothes.

My mother left him when I was 15. They didn't have much of a marriage by then. I wanted her to have a life.

So what happened to my father? From then on, he drifted into stop gap, month-to-month jobs, living on his small Army pension. He died in the late 1950s.

Yet here was a man who had graduated with honors from the University of Pennsylvania's Wharton School in 1904, one of the men most likely to succeed. He had leads in the university's Mask and Wig Club. He was handsome and charming when my mother fell in love with him.

So why, unlike her, did he give up when the Depression cast its pall over the country? All these years it has bothered me. Who was this man?

Recently, my brother found a copy of our father's hand-written resume.

I found out he did try jobs. That made me feel better.

His vita reads like something between Clint Eastwood movies and an F. Scott Fitzgerald story.

After he graduated from college, he worked in coal mines from West Virginia to Mexico, as a toll taker at the St. Louis World's Fair, a construction worker in the Philippines and a cowhand in Wyoming.

Then between 1910 and 1920, he came home and was "an investment banker." (Ah, those must have been the married years when he stayed put.) Beginning in 1918, he was a captain in the Army for a couple of years. But, because he was a Quaker, he did not go overseas.

The next line, in bold caps, was "1929, The Depression!"

After that, he waited for some big company to call him and offer him an executive job. His pride got in his way.

And I feel sorry for him, even now.

What I liked about recently finding him out was that he was an adventurer of sorts — coal mines, bridges, the West. Those were the days when Philadelphians didn't venture west of the Mississippi.

My mother told me once when I asked what went wrong that he wanted to get away from his staid Philadelphia family and be an actor, a musician.

In his last years, he got his wish, living alone in a boarding house, playing the piano at a restaurant and bar near Valley Forge. I saw him last there playing "Stardust" and his own rendition of "Red Sails in the Sunset" and accepting free drinks. He was content, and I was glad for him.

For my brother and me perhaps he was the consummate actor, because we never knew the real man inside. That's acting, isn't it?

But my father's life taught me this: that one does have to work, that one does not give up, that there is always someone out there who counts on you. He found a way to break away, but he missed us in doing so. And we missed a father.

A Few Dos and Some Don'ts
for Grannies and Nannies

In my handbook for new grandmothers that I have not written yet, I will try to make grannies and nannies feel like life not only begins at 40, but it also positively grooves when that first grandchild is born.

My book, entitled "The Making of the Grandmother," will praise this high echelon of "mothers emeritus," who deserve a lot of credit.

Gone are your worries about the dimpled fat on your inner thighs, those brown spots on your hands, the wrinkles under your chin. Gone is the envy over your 45-year-old friend who looks good in a bikini. You can finally relax and say, "I'm a grandmother."

But those little worries are immediately replaced with worry over whether they are feeding the new baby the best formula. Are they burping the baby halfway through the bottle? Is the cat jumping up in the crib?

The "they" is that sweet, in-love couple, one of whom is related to you, and who promised to love, honor and obey each other (but not their parents anymore) during that beautiful recent-ceremony-that-your-husband-just-finished-paying-for.

The pregnancy came off all right without your daily presence. She even had the baby without your being there.

But now this precious bundle is theirs, not yours, and you have to learn to share. You are only the grandmother.

Now some don'ts: Don't call every night between 5 and 6, because that's the baby's crying time, and you might want to rush right over; don't call between 5 a.m. and 9 a.m., because modern babies seem to sleep longer in the morning than your babies did, or, worse, the baby might answer the phone and tell you her mother is asleep! Don't call between 9 a.m. and noon because she is trying to bathe the baby without you, or she is trying to wash diapers with those newfangled pre-soaks.

In fact don't call at all — they'll call you.

Don't, whatever you do, tell them how you used to bathe, dress or feed your babies. And above all, don't say things to them like, "Now your great-grandmother used to boil the bottles with a pinch of salt and soda."

When you see them take the new baby out in 6-degree weather, don't say anything — just smile and say, "Babies are so much hardier today." I mean, have you ever heard of a frozen baby in a middle-class family in America?

Don't tell them that those paper diapers are giving the baby diaper rash, and that his rear end looks like W.C. Fields' nose. In fact, smile a lot. Nothing gives these kids more confidence than your smile. I mean, do you want to be known as the "scary" granny, the dominating, interfering grandmother, or the popular granny?

As an award-winning granny, you will overhear them saying, "Golly, your mom never interferes." You may never hear it — or by the time you do, you'll be deaf.

Now, about your clothes as a new grandmother. Don't dress too young, or they won't think you are mature enough to babysit. Miniskirts, see-through blouses and eye makeup — that's out. Look loose, somewhere between Whistler's mother and Phyllis Diller.

Don't compare anything genetically. I mean, don't look at the baby's toes when the parents aren't looking and say, "Oh, she has beautiful toes, just like Aunt Ginny's." Be sure to acknowledge the fact that the baby could have pretty teeth from her daddy's side.

When they ask you if it's OK to feed the baby duck at 6 months, don't look surprised, give a definite answer, never fence straddle.

You must remember there's a new world coming in discipline. When you buy the baby his first coloring book and crayons and the mother says, "Granny, we don't let Junior have coloring books, it destroys his creativity — he shouldn't have to color within the lines," don't laugh. Hold it until he draws all over his bedroom walls with Crayolas.

And when he's 4 and still not potty trained, don't be shocked when they say, "Mom, we don't want to inhibit him, you know." (Don't laugh when he is sent home soaked during the first-grade Lincoln's Birthday play.)

The joys of grandmotherhood are many. You might as well relax and enjoy every stage. Because deep in your heart you know that someday that precious bundle smelling of baby powder will grow up to be terrible 2, fidgety 4, sassy 5 — and lastly a belligerent, rebellious teen-ager who will look at you as if you were an Egyptian mummy, a decaying artifact, a historical thing — from another world!

Be Thankful if the
Married Children Show Up At All

When you sit down to your Thanksgiving meal, you can bet on two things: If it's at your house, you've gone to a lot of trouble for something that disappears in less than an hour, and some of those children who are now married have had a real marital rhubarb about whether they should be there at all.

To turkey or not to turkey? Where to turkey? To chicken out in the end?

What I mean is that married couples who have not had an altercation in months may find themselves torn asunder over the question of where to have Thanksgiving dinner.

The decision can have in-law fallout for years to come if they don't show up (or even if they show and are mad and moody). Making the decision is more difficult if both sets of parents live within driving distance. I mean, if one set lives in Disaster, Wyo., and the other in Cross Roads, Mass., then you just go to the parents nearest you, right?

I overheard Pam and Jeff trying to decide. There are many Pams and Jeffs across the country, and they are usually nice and amiable. But holidays put extra pressure on the best of relationships.

Pam: "I think we should go to my parents for Thanksgiving this year. We went to your parents' house last year, remember? Your mother made me take the yucky frozen stuff out of the turkey, and then she refolded the napkins I'd already put on the table. I'll never forget."

Jeff: "Wait a minute, we went to your parents for Christmas. And your father made me bring in all the wood, and it had tar on it, and I got it all over my new suit. And the reason Mother asked you to take those frozen things out is that you had once said in a fit of in-law buttering that you liked giblet gravy."

Pam: "Well, this year, I don't think I'm up to hearing your sisters argue with your father over Ronald Reagan."

Jeff: "Well, what about your father always bringing up Prohibition and marijuana? You might think he was smoking it, he gets so weird. That's all he can talk about. And besides, they always have sauerkraut, and I hate sauerkraut."

And on and on it goes, the pre-holiday litany of discord.

Well, I have suggested to Pam and Jeff how to solve this diplomatically.

You can do what we used to do when we lived in the same city with both sets of parents. You just go to both families for Thanksgiving dinner. You just make sure that one is having dinner at 5 and the other at 8. We managed one Thanksgiving to eat an entire turkey and ham dinner at 3:30 in the afternoon, and then again at 8 in the evening.

You just eat a little of this and a little of that. But very little. You wear loose clothes. You fast three days prior to the holiday. Take plenty of bi-carb with you. And don't let on that you are double dipping.

But two things are very important:

Don't touch the wine until you get to the second set of parents, because it can increase your appetite.

And for heaven's sake don't say anything foolish like "Pass the turkey," or "Gee, this pie is great," or "May I have the recipe?" This just brings on a deluge of seconds, and that could end up being, in Valley terms, a real barf out.

Eating twice is a small price to pay for peace.

Take a Stroll — Jog Bittersweet Memories

I found out another thing girls do better than boys. They know how to stroll. The art of strolling is a pastime that has almost been forgotten. You have to watch closely to see it. Boys stand on street corners and ogle or they ride fast bikes, but young girls, especially in small towns, still stroll.

You remember strolling or leisurely walking? Shakespeare wrote about it. Mark Twain talked about it.

People used to do it in cities before people turned on people in the streets and parks. People used to stroll before people carried transistor radios and tennis rackets or ran in running shoes or jumped on motorbikes.

Perhaps it's more the fact that we cannot take the time to stroll, to meander, because we are so busy going about our business or someone else's business.

I was in a small town last week and I saw two young girls strolling. Little girls can teach us much, if we'd just watch and listen. School is out, and they are not tainted by pressures and fears.

One looked to be about 12 and one was younger. They would giggle, walk, skip and stroll. And my heart ached for the old days of sitting on the front porch glider and watching the neighbors stroll by on a hot summer night. Or strolling down the city sidewalks and looking into the windows at things we couldn't afford. Or the summer days when people made ice cream in the backyard. Nostalgia. My theater of longing.

I followed the two little girls for a few blocks. What do little girls talk about today while they are strolling?

The talk was almost the same as it was long ago. If I could have closed my eyes, I was back then, way back when.

"Didn't Mary look dumb at the party. What was that dumb dress? ... I hope I don't get Mr. Firthby next year for math. ..."

They stopped to talk to a boy who was painting his fence. They stopped to watch a moving van unload. They stopped to pick up a pretty pebble or stone or to pull some honeysuckle off a vine.

"Is your mother going to let you go to the beach Friday?"

"Darn it, no. She said no."

Then, "Look at Mrs. Pringle, she's in that upstairs window. She looks like a ghost. Her house is haunted, you know. I found out. Look quick."

"She is a ghost, one night. ..." the other said, as she lowered her voice.

And then I knew I'd stepped back in time, back to when kids made up their own fantasies and did not have to see them electronically. I was a ghost from the 1940s and 1950s for a few minutes, deja vuing. I wanted to tell them "Hi," but they might have been told, "Don't talk to strangers."

It was a small friendly town, but it was still the summer of '81.

I walked away, but not before I saw their Mrs. Pringle. Yes, she did look like a ghost, and if I were 12 again, I'd try to find out, too.

So take the time to stroll this summer, and look around you. As the song goes, "You gotta stop and smell the roses."

Or maybe you gotta find a summer ghost.

Grandmother, What Big Memories You Have

Grandmother sits on the patio, the part of the grass that used to be called the back yard of the suburban house. She is sitting in the old swing, which used to be hung from an old porch ceiling, and sipping her iced tea.

She is looking back in time, wistfully, somewhat fitfully.

Back then, she would fly in armed with new children's books and games and stories filed away in her head, stories they were eager to hear before television took audiences away. Somehow, they liked to hear the tales over and over. Now, they were too old for her version of "Jack and the Beanstalk" and too young for "A Midsummer Night's Dream."

The grandmother did this babysitting stint every summer for each of her married children so they could get away from their own small children for a small vacation. It was a gift of love, and she loved giving it.

She is sitting trying to read a new book, but the place is too quiet. Now the children are teen-agers, and she is lonely. One is at softball practice and another is taking a summer-school exam.

Where have the years flown? And why did they go by so fast?

She remembers singing them to sleep on this same swing. She remembers the old seesaw they made together. She remembers the spare Barbie doll she was given when she played Barbie with them, right here on this same spot, with cardboard boxes for the houses. She remembers cuddling them on the sofa while reading aloud a book of fairy tales. She remembers the fall her grandson took while he was in her care and the trip to the hospital to get the five stitches. And how that incident drew them closer.

Her granddaughter's room has no more Barbie things. It is wall-to-wall posters of the Rage, the Rolling Stones and other rock groups. Trays of makeup are piled up on her bureau. The boy's room, which was once chock full of Legos, is full of acoustical equipment. He plays the guitar.

They come home. Smiling, hot and tired. And she asks the usual questions: How was school? How was the ballgame? And although they are polite, it is as if a scrim cloth has been dropped between them and her. They answer in monosyllables. They can't wait to get to the phone.

They are beautiful children, and she loves them. But they are beginning to drift away from her and parentland to weave their own lives. And the grandmother wonders: What role should she play now? She wants to communicate, but she can't cuddle anymore.

She has cooked their favorite dinner, a request: spaghetti and meatballs.

Suddenly, something hits the grandmother like a ton of Legos.

"Listen, kids, how would you like to go out for dinner? You two get to pick the place."

They are ecstatic. The grandmother puts away for another night the already-cooked meal.

"No kidding, Gran, that's great."

"Let's celebrate summer, OK? Go get dressed up."

The restaurant is called the Mad Hatter, and it is fancy and they have all dressed up for the event. And the grandmother finds out the way to a teenager's soul is, maybe, through his or her stomach. Her granddaughter says, "Nana, this is super. And what's more, Jane and Pammy have never been here. ..." Those are her best friends.

They laugh and they talk. They tell her strange and new things. They are the storytellers now. Finally, she feels part of them again. It is suddenly like old times.

The waiter leans over and tells the grandmother, "You have beautiful children."

And that did it for the grandmother.

"Kids, we must come here more often."

And summer, with its family banner, marches on for all of them. A Midsummer Night's Dream come true.

When the Boy Becomes a Man

He's sitting opposite me in a three-piece suit filled with business cards, credit cards and an upscale pen and pencil set, and he's picking at a lobster.

He once sat opposite me in a high chair in a Virginia restaurant picking at a plate of green beans and french fries with his fingers. Oh, how time flies.

All grandparents, indeed, all parents hope for the time when their children or grandchildren grow up and become people of substance.

Was there a time when you didn't think your teen-ager was going to grow up and be part of the real world? Sure.

He had called from his car phone. He was in the area and wanted to take me to lunch. He'd never taken me to lunch, and he'd never had a car of his own, much less a car phone.

He's our first grandchild. He is now 22 and into his first "big boy" job, a good job with an expense account, base pay and all the perks. He got the position right out of college. This can't be happening, I tell myself. Is he really that old?

"You pick your favorite restaurant, Gran," he says. "I'll pick you up at noon."

I sit there and look at him. Do you remember as a parent how every now and then you would look at your child and say, "How would I perceive him if I weren't related?" Or "Will he become all the things we hope he will become?"

I am doing that now, sitting across the table from him.

If he came into a room full of people, would I single him out?

Yes, I think I would. He is handsome and has a certain sophistication.

The business suit with the "power" tie is just right. He carries a briefcase, and his shoes are shined.

He is also well-built, thanks to weightlifting, the tennis team and a host of other sports that cost his parents plenty through the years.

You could say I am prejudiced, of course, and that my opinions are slanted by the weight of love.

He scans the wine list as I look on and remember the baby who 21 years ago threw spaghetti on the floor in a restaurant that fortunately had a red carpet.

Is this the same baby whose diaper I changed while he wriggled like a newly hooked bass on the line?

Is this the child who fell on a step at my house while visiting and had to be taken to the emergency room? I was frantic; his parents were wonderful.

Is this the same boy who always asked for a new guitar at Christmas and would bribe us with chores to garner the money?

Is this the child who, at the beach, tried surfing with his small board, over and over, never catching a wave? After three hours, with nobody but his grandmother to see, he finally caught a wave. He was 11 and victorious. I was exhausted from worry.

Is this the same boy with whom I had to sit for hours one long night and go over his science notes so he would pass the test, and he still didn't pass?

Is this the same kid whom I would worry about because at noon on a summer day he was still asleep? I'd forgotten that he'd been up late with his friends playing rock music and that youth can simply turn the world off and sleep.

Is this the same boy who loved beer at 16, even though I told him it's really fattening and addictive?

Is this the child who brought home his first girlfriend — the one who wore so much makeup my husband remarked, "Maybe she's a clown in the circus"?

Remembering how many times we ate pizza together, I am now appalled that I am ordering an expensive smoked salmon.

There was only one unsure moment, when he kind of fiddled with the credit card bill.

"Let me get the tip," I suggested.

"Of course not, Gran," he says. "I charge it all."

And I see his math is as bad as mine, because it takes him a few minutes to figure out the tip while the waiter looks on smiling.

And finally my jitters turn to pride, because he left a 20 percent tip, which is, after all, a very nice thing to do.

Child-to-man: The amazing, maturing metamorphosis, and, remarkably, I got to watch.

Reading List for an Infant

I can't believe it, but I am reading to a 10-month-old baby. We are on our backs on his parents' big double bed while his mother has gone to the grocery store.

He is sucking on his pacifier, grinning and fighting sleep. I am trying not to fall asleep while reading a book that his mom recommended from his reading list. It's called "Goodnight Moon," and she says it is one of his favorites and makes him sleepy.

I wish I had a pacifier.

He does like the book! He laughs when I turn to a new page. What does that tell us about his early IQ? I dunno, you tell me.

He's just the cutest thing you've ever seen — this from his grandmother's point of view. He is now "bicycling' with his short, fat legs, and I am thinking I should be bicycling with my fat, longer legs too, while we read.

As an older grandchild commented on her new cousin, "Babies sure don't do much, do they?"

Well, hon, it's just a matter of time. Just you wait and see. Right now, we should be glad he's not going for the light switches or car keys, and shoving his teddy bear in the toilet.

Anyway, after "Moon," we read "Runaway Bunny," and he laughs some more. Then I get a little bored and wonder if he has "Green Eggs and Ham," one of my old favorites. Or would he like Russell Baker's new book, "The Good Times," that I have brought with me to read when he goes to sleep.

"Hey," I tell him, "my book has pictures."

He does not respond, so we read "Moon" again. I now know it by heart.

He has started a kind of high whine, which means ... He's wet? He wants to go to sleep? He wants a bottle? He wants me to read "Runaway Bunny" again?

I do, I read it four more times, and he is now starting a mild fussing.

There was a recent "Cosby" show in which one of the older girls in the Huxtable family baby-sat her sister's twins, and she had to play a tape of "I've Been Working on the Railroad," their favorite song, according to the parents, in order to get the twins to sleep.

I ask him what he wants me to sing.

He stares at me with his big, brown eyes, just like his father does when I ask him the preposterous question, "Do you want a second helping of key lime pie?" The baby smiles, but I can tell he wants action.

OK, a signal to activate my voice box. I start with "Old MacDonald Had a Farm." He does not like it, and I'm getting mixed up with the verses, which could be why he does not like it. So I sing, "Frere Jacques."

Did he ever go to sleep before his mother came home? Sure he did, but not before I changed him, gave him a bottle, put him in his familiar crib, patted him gently a few times and said "Goodnight Moon" and hummed a few bars of Brahms and "Frere Jacques."

Then I went back and threw myself on the bed with Russell Baker and a stupid, steamy romance novel, read a while, then snoozed until his mother appeared with her groceries.

Sure, I should have been cleaning her oven for her or rearranging her spice shelf, instead of napping. But that's the great part of grandmothering. You can turn the chores off while baby-sitting and finish a book.

Which is something you never got to do when you were the "prime parent," right?

Did my own babies look that cute when they were sleeping? I don't remember, because I probably had to bake a cake for the PTA, whip up a casserole, make a bas relief map out of paste for a fourth-grader or vacuum while they slept.

A Grandmother's Loving Reflections

Here I am, sitting in the oak rocker that is older than I am, feeling very good indeed.

In April I rocked a few times in this same rocker — just to practice — then I wrote about the anticipation of waiting for a baby.

Now I'm back, my first time baby-sitting the new baby while his mother, my daughter, is out running errands.

Back and forth I rock, just like before, but where once I wondered, "What, if and who will he be?" now I have him in my arms — a soft, sweet-smelling bundle of life.

Ah, the miracle of birth.

He is beautiful to us, but then we are his family.

He had just been fed, and he ought to be sleeping. But, instead, his big, brown eyes, like his daddy's, are open wide, staring straight up at me as if to say, "Who are you anyway?

Although we are surrounded by many baby clothes and other accouterments (mobiles, toys, books, new curtains and matching crib sheets), this day he is in just a diaper and a receiving blanket, which seems to be his favorite outfit. He's happily unencumbered by designer labels and other adult frills.

He was two weeks late coming into the world, which, to me, makes him all the more precious.

So I am singing "Baa Baa Black Sheep" and "Jingle Bells" and anything that has a slightly high pitch to it. He also seems to like arias from *Carmen*.

Back and forth I rock while one tiny hand clasps mine. What a comparison: his hands are soft, his fingers so perfectly unmarried; mine are spotted brown, slightly gnarled and old. He doesn't have much hair, so I wonder what he will look like with hair. What color will it be? There is peach fuzz on his new cheeks.

I'm trying to pretend he looks like someone in either of the parents' families and I know he doesn't — he looks like himself. I am also trying to pretend I remember which is the back and the front on these new disposable diapers. Do the little ducks go at the back? I've never worked Velcro tabs before.

So much serenity surrounds us in this room. I tell him how glad I am that he is finally here, how much I love him and how I can't wait until he can talk to me and walk with me.

Then I think how silly — we want them to be perfect, of course. We push them into turning over, crawling, walking and finally talking, communicating with us. Then when they do all that, we realize they can be a lot of trouble, that they have to be monitored every waking minute, and we have to discipline them and tell them, "no, no."

And here I am projecting when I should be gathering every baby minute from this bundle of cuteness. So today I don't have to do anything but bond with him.

Oh, I know I am running on like a new grandmother, but don't you do the same thing with a new baby?

I'm 60-something and he's my fourth grandchild. Suddenly a chill comes over me. Will I be here when he goes to first grade?

Yes, please, yes. Let me live to show him how to ride a two-wheeler. Let me be around to hear about his first day at school. Let me live to read him "Green Eggs and Ham" and "Charlotte's Web."

I rock slower now. His eyes are trying to close, but he fights it. I think he just smiled because I am singing a lullaby. But I don't flatter myself. That's not the reason he is going to sleep now, it is just me.

I wash away my thoughts of old age with the rhythm of the rocker, and I remember that I must tell his mother that some of his baby hair is falling out. No, I remind myself, I promise not to tell her anything unless she asks. He is their baby, and grandparents must be careful.

Both his eyes are closed now.

It would be nice if time could stand still.

Generations with No Gap

The tall and tanned 20-year-old is smiling as she bridges the distance to the 14-month-old baby. The baby, his arms outstretched, his chubby hands splayed to hold his balance on the uneven sand, is waddling as fast as he can toward the young woman.

They are two of my grandchildren who had not seen each other for six months. The baby probably doesn't really remember his older cousin. But something intuitive tells him she is family, that she is safe and is going to hug him.

They make contact and she picks him up and swings him in the air. Giggles ensue.

This is what being a grandmother means, watching the grandchildren bond.

I am full of joy, for they will get to know one another here at our annual ocean trek, where sea, sand and spray make our world look benign and where three generations come together.

I watch the reunion.

I hope for time to stand still and for a fleeting two minutes, I gather up my hungry thoughts like a fish net swooping up the catch of the day.

I let the sweetness of the moment permeate my vacation mode — the baby so trusting, the young woman with so much love to give.

My granddaughter is home from college and is geared for relaxation with the family, while he, as a year old, is celebrating the fact that he can walk, if wobbly, by himself.

I realize I am looking at a generation span.

And more shocking for me suddenly is the thought that I might not live to see him graduate from high school as I did her — after all, I am 60-plus.

I remember how I taught her catchy tunes, songs from my day, how to play jacks, how to ride a two-wheeler, how to enjoy the varied faces of the pansy and the mysterious intricacies of the snapdragon. And I realize that I might not be able to do those things with him.

I have tears in my eyes — they are self-serving tears — because with the older grandchildren I had some input as they went from babyhood to teen-agers.

Oh, the tyranny of time.

And I realize my vulnerability.

Time, of course, will take me from them, but here is a redeeming thought. And I go with it.

My 20-year-old grandchild will be there when he graduates from college. She'll applaud him and support him. She will be 40 and I laugh.

What a splendid and wonderful notion to contemplate now — the young taking over when the older ones give out.

Shall I run out there and tell her to see to it that he wears nice shoes under his graduating gown? That he reads Dickens' "The Forsythe Saga," the Old Testament, uses the dictionary? And please see that he knows where Sri Lanka is; that Helena is the capital of Montana; and that Wilmington is not the capital of Delaware, but Dover is; that he helps others and tries to fix the world, or at least the space around him — all the small things that I tried to ingrain in my own children.

Sure, she will be there for him, and that is why the procreation and continuation of family is important.

On second thought, time isn't so tyrannous — it is just too fleeting.

Now I feel good, I am sustained and I won't set timetables, for that's tempting fate.

Ecclesiastes has it right: " … a time to weep, and a time to laugh, a time to mourn, and a time to dance."

And I am now happy just to dance.

Noise, Clutter Make a Home

It was at a cookout that I heard the talk.

One young woman with two children said, "I wish we could afford a bigger house, or at least new dining room furniture."

Her friend with a 2-year-old said, "I know, we've just got to get a garage. Our house has just no storage, we are so crowded. ..."

From then on, they all talked about what they wanted and what they didn't have.

And I know their longing stems from the heart. I know that when you work hard and have children, you want a return on your labors. I also remember when I was 25 and longed for a four-bedroom house. I had four children and a visiting mother. I never got the extra bedrooms.

I understand the feeling for things. And yes, things can make your life better, but they don't always make it best.

On the way home from the cookout, I got to thinking about a house I loved so much. I have never been back to it since we moved away from that small Western town, but even now it can make me tear up. The past doesn't always recede.

When I see a picture of it, even in my mind's eye, a deep hurtful nostalgia washes over me. I loved that place, and I have lived many places. I am still homesick for that small house, our first, and one that was usually bulging with people. And I long for it more in the summer for some reason, maybe because it had large windows that brought the Western sunshine inside

The house was made of tacky asbestos siding and had an ugly carport that was full of bikes, broken lawn mowers and kids' toys — the house was small.

I try not to look back. I realize my longings are for something that once was and will never be again.

How immature of me to have a flight of fantasy. I live in a nice house now; it has air conditioning, a garbage disposal, a fireplace and flower beds. The children are grown, and we are alone. We have what 30- and 40-year-old parents long for — peace.

We have matching dining room chairs now, but they are not filled with children day after day.

I know what my trouble is: The house of 37 years ago is the house in which we started out. We were very crowded, and when my mother came to stay for a few months at a time, we were more crowded.

We had no family room. We lived in our living room. The kids shared rooms, and there was no privacy.

But that old house had constant laughter, continuous loud music, the telephone ringing, coats thrown over chairs, cars parked outside. Spaces were filled with kids of all ages. We didn't care.

And sure, there were occasional spats. Popcorn, an open peanut butter jar and cheap perfume from the girls' rooms mingled with the weird lint fragrance of the old clothes dryer that labored every day.

I wish I could tell young people who long for better houses that a new deck, another bathroom and larger kitchens are not always the things that make a house a home. It's the loved ones inside who bring about the theater of happiness and keep the daily drama moving.

Even the constant banging of the always-off-the-track screened door is now a sweet memory.

And today I am wondering if the yucca is in bloom in the scraggy back yard of that old house.

But most of all, a shout after school at the front door, sometimes sullen, sometimes joyous, "Mom, I'm home!" brings back a yearning.

That was living. That's what I think I miss most.

Chapter 11

Twinkle, twinkle, Christmas Star

Christmas Dream of Help For All

I had this dream last night.

I was taking a 5-year-old to see Santa Claus.

There was a sign over Santa's throne. It said, "Ask not what you want for Christmas, and tell me what you can give."

How strange, I thought. Then I heard them.

There was a cute, little boy of about 7, who said he's giving all his piggy bank savings to Santa Claus Anonymous.

Then there was a little girl, about 5, who told Santa she was giving her mom three housecleanings for Christmas.

Another small boy said he was giving his daddy a car wash and 10 shoe shines.

Some of the little people told Santa they were giving their used toys away.

Then came a big boy of 10. And he said, "Santa Claus, I know I'm too old to come see you, but I thought I'd drop by to tell you about the starving kids in Bangladesh and Africa and the kids here in the orphanages and hospitals — could you help them?"

"Wait a minute, sonny," Santa said, "I'm just one old man. I can't drive those reindeer that far in one night. But let's see, if I had some help, perhaps I could wake up the world when I fly over the roof tops.

"Imagine a little hope, faith and love spreading everywhere. That would be some kind of Christmas," he added with a twinkle in his eye. It would be the merriest Christmas, wouldn't it?"

And then I woke up from my dream. And there were tears in my eyes.

Christmas — Through the Eyes of a Child

A 5-year-old boy was shopping with me in a crowded department store. His little hand was damp with excitement as it clenched mine. We were going to see Santa Claus, and he was scared.

As we waited in the long line, he said, "Granny, is Santa related to Jesus Christ?"

"No, not at all, why?"

"But they always come around about the same time of year. Jesus in his funny-looking manger and Santa in that beautiful red velvet throne in the store. ... I get mixed up."

Then I tried to explain. "You see, Jesus came over 2,000 years ago, he was, for the Christian world, the son of God, the prince of peace, and that's why we celebrate Christmas every year. It's his birthday. You remember that."

"Oh, sure, I do," the child answered, "but, Granny, it's too bad Jesus can't come again and talk to Santa. Think of all the things he could tell Santa to do. ..."

"Like what, Tad?"

"Like maybe they could get more food for hungry kids, like a new arm for Jackie Saunders, because his is crippled, or more clothes for some of those kids in the war that I see on TV ... and maybe if they didn't mind, a 10-speed bike for Andy, then I could learn to ride one."

"Why don't you mention those things to Santa?"

"Oh, no, Granny, you're funny," he said as he wiggled his little feet and pulled his car coat hood over his laughing face. "He'd think I was a baby."

"No, he wouldn't, Tad, he'd know you were a man, a real man."

When You Wish Upon a Star ...

During the early years of our marriage, I received sheets for Christmas because we needed them.

Then there was the year I got snow tires because we needed them.

And when times were better, I was surprised with pretty blouses, night-gowns, robes and jewelry.

But the best years of all were the years when the children were young. I received such gifts as handmade match boxes covered with carefully pasted sequins or an empty bleach bottle made into a piggy bank with a pipe cleaner tail.

And I remember an orange juice can decorated with yarn and holding used pencils.

The most memorable Christmas present of all I received long ago, from the oldest of our four children, when she was in kindergarten.

It is a six-pointed, slightly lopsided, cardboard star. It is outlined in gold paint, "Peace on Earth, Goodwill Toward Men" is written in blue crayon in the center.

We haven't put the star on the tree every year, because we were afraid it might crumble. What's more, some of our Christmas trees were too small for that star.

But I think it's time to get it out again for this year.

So I've unpacked the star from the decoration box and carefully unwrapped it from the fading tissue paper.

And I'm putting it on top of the tree for the grandchildren to see.

There's still, years later, not much peace on earth and very little goodwill toward men.

Yet a mother can never stop hoping.

And a star can never stop reaching out.

It's the Thought That Counts

Don't ever underestimate the power of children from 8 to 20 to amuse themselves during the lull that follows the holidays.

They were seated around the table regaling themselves with a game called "What was the worst present I received?"

Samples: "My worst gift was a pair of 100 percent polyester green slacks that I get every Christmas from the same person. ... I got a hand-knit sweater with one arm five inches longer than the other. ... I got a dust pan and laundry basket. ... I got a battery-operated single-egg scrambler. ... I got a box of cookies loaded with anise, and the sugar was left out. ... I got a bottle of chianti that had fermented. ... I got a plastic reindeer full of terrible cologne, which I poured down the john.

"My dumbest gift was a black velvet painting of Elvis Presley. ... I got a trick puzzle that no one can do. ... I got a crocheted potholder, and I can't cook. ... Uncle Fred sent me "Moby Dick" again. ... I got a ceramic Santa that winds up and sings something, but I don't know what. ... I got a necktie that the dog barks at," and on and on it went. I tried to top them. I told them about the Christmas of 1959, when I received spark plugs in a gift box, and, as I remember, I cried. But I told them it's not the gift but the thought that counts.

And then they told me they thought a box of spanking new spark plugs was a thoughtful gift. Then I told them they ought to make a New Year's resolution that it is "more blessed to give than to gripe."

Then they told me they wish they'd received some new spark plugs instead of useless objects.

Then I told them never look a gift horse in the mouth, unless you can return the horse, gracefully.

Today's Little Dears Won't Buy the Hype

There is simply nothing more exciting than taking the kids to see Santa Claus. Right? I mean, that's as American as Ronald Reagan, Ronald McDonald, tacos and apple pie.

There's just nothing like seeing the little kids' faces light up. And hearing them scream when Santa takes them up on his lap, because for years Mom has said, "Don't take candy from a strange man."

I took five children to see Santa the other day. Their ages were 9, 8, 7 and two 5-year-olds. Some weren't related to me. I had been looking forward to it all weekend.

To show you how excited they were, when we went through the lovely store that was festively decked out for the holidays, I said, "Aren't the decorations beautiful this year?" The 10-year-old answered me with a question, "Where's the record shop in this mall?"

Well, Santa turned out to be two beguiling, but mechanical, "talking" reindeer.

I was thrilled. How innovative. And besides, one had a girl voice and one had a man voice so that in this unisex world, all would be appeased.

We shoved the two 5-year-olds, Mark and Bobby, up to the deer, as I figured they were the only ones who still believed in Santa Claus.

The man deer said very gently to Mark, "And what do you want for Christmas, little boy?"

Mark said, very sweetly, "A Boeing 747."

And the other said, "A nuclear submarine."

Then Mark told the deer, "You aren't real, you know, you are electronic." And as if that weren't enough, when the girl deer laughed a kind of tinkly nervous laugh, Mark added, "I'll bet you aren't married to her."

By now, the crowd was laughing.

I thought, what's with these kids? They are questioning those darling deer. They were, of course, being too smart. Right then, I decided that these children were too advanced for trips to Santa. So I took them away from the deer and the live audience, who thought they were funny, to the soda bar, where the children then discussed the technique used to amplify the deer's voices.

And I thought to myself, rather sadly, that it was my fault they were really too old to be snowed by "talking" deer and to believe in Santa. They are children of the new world, the new wave. They are blasé, spoiled and over-achieved. There's a paucity of simple fantasy in their modern realm.

But we love them, and that might see them through.

I remembered how much fun Santa used to be in our day. And then I wondered if there is any way to bring that spirit back.

So, to all talking deer everywhere, take heart, with hope we can entice the new-wave child to believe in something. Even if it's just himself or herself.

Christmas is Whenever the Time is Right

It was Christmas Eve, 1945. Three Navy wives sat on a sunny beach at Coronado, Calif., laughing, talking and waiting. A game they'd played before: keeping their spirits up. One was from Atlanta, one was from St. Louis, one was from Philadelphia. They were all in their 20s, recently married. "War brides," they called them then.

They were waiting for an aircraft carrier. Not just any aircraft carrier, but the one that their husbands were on, and had been on for months. War was on with Japan.

They wanted more than anything else to have Christmas with their husbands, even if it was in a hotel room in San Diego.

There had been this rumor: "The ship is coming in. The captain's wife lives in San Diego, and he wants to spend Christmas at home."

Then there was another rumor: "The ship is just qualifying squadrons off the harbor, it would be in on Christmas Eve."

Then there was another rumor: "The ship is through qualifying squadrons, and it is headed for battle to take up its position with the 7th Fleet. The ship would not be in for Christmas."

For the young girl from Philadelphia, it was the loneliest Christmas she could remember. She was the youngest of the three wives, only 20. Her longing was terrible. Back home, her mother, her sisters and the family were starting to gather around the large Christmas tree. She could almost smell a Philadelphia Christmas and hear the sounds — the pine boughs, the baking, the carols — and she could imagine the snow covering the trees. An open fire would be burning on the hearth even if there was no snow. The terrible longing.

The Navy wives laughed, talked and waited. The game. The waiting, a thing they had learned to do pretty well over the last few months. But in this game, no one seemed to win.

The girl from Philadelphia bought a small fake tree, all that was available in the area at the time. She propped it up in an open drawer of the hotel bureau. She decorated it with cheap things, just in case.

Christmas Eve came and went. Christmas Day came and went. But the day after Christmas, the mighty ship rounded the corner of the harbor. A two-day leave was granted. They celebrated Christmas. It was beautiful.

And the girl from Philadelphia and her young husband found out, like so many other people, that Christmas can be celebrated anytime, really. Dec. 26 is OK for Christmas; almost any day can be Christmas if you just know how to remember.

Christmas is in the heart and soul. It can't be masked by war or fear.

The couple is older and wiser now, and they still remember that, above all, Christmas is love and hope.

Even today, they remember the Christmas that fell on Dec. 26. Like any anniversary, Christmas could be forever if only we would let it.

Portrait on Their Christmas Card? Forget It

This year, we decided to get back at all our friends who, over the years, have sent us family portraits printed on their Christmas cards. Our attempt backfired — but not for lack of effort.

We have received cards in which the mother and father look great, but the 2-year-old is sticking out his tongue and the 4-year-old has his finger in his nose.

Or we've received pictures where the mother looked so worn out we wondered if she'd make it until Christmas. Did she just have major surgery?

Last year, we received a picture from a family in Oregon, who were proud to announce they now have 10 children. The mother was seated in the middle of a padded rocking chair and looked like she'd been crying.

"I wonder where Jake is?" I asked my husband. (Jake's the father.) "You don't suppose he ..."

"No, dummy, he was taking the picture."

So he was. Jake mentioned this in his 25-page, mimeographed Christmas newsletter to us — and hundreds of others.

We received another picture from a childless couple in Texas, whom we had not seen in years. They had their arms around each other and had posed under the mistletoe. The brief, accompanying note said they were now happily divorced.

Yes, their picture must have been taken a bit too early.

So we plotted our Christmas card way ahead of time. The kids wanted us all to climb an evergreen tree in the back yard. "That would be Christmasy," they said.

Eddie, our good friend and mailman, said he'd come by and take the picture. He'd been a photographer for the police department.

But let me tell you that posing four children and the grandchildren for a family picture on a hot summer day was like preparing untrained troops for a full-scale war.

Four-year-old: "I don't want to sit next to Tommy. He smells bad."

Father to a son: "Run in and take a few inches off your hair, buddy."

Teen-ager to teen-ager: "Don't smile, your braces will show."

Grandchild: "I want to be on the front line or I won't play."

Another grandchild: "If I can't hold my guinea pig, I won't be in the picture."

Twenty-eight-year-old: "Wait, I've got to go change wigs."

Twenty-two-year-old girl: "Please put me in the back row on account of my legs."

Finally, the father took command. "Look, we're going to pose like the Roosevelt family used to. I'll sit in the middle, the patriarch. And mother, you stand beside me and lovingly place your hand on my shoulder.

"You kids remember this is no beauty contest. Just shut up and sit. When I count to three, everyone try to smile."

"Wait!" I yelled. "Where's Eddie? I thought he was going to take the picture?"

"Oh no, I forgot to call him. Well, he'll be here in 20 minutes to deliver the mail. Everyone just sit still."

Eddie tried, but by then the subject matter had completely disintegrated. The pictures were so bad we won't be using them on our Christmas card.

Aren't you glad?

A Poor Boy on the Street
at Christmas is No Fable

"The Little Match Girl" by Hans Christian Andersen, circa 1840. Christmas. "It was dreadfully cold. It was snowing, and the evening was beginning to darken. Through the cold and the dark, the poor little girl with bare head and naked feet was wandering along the road. ... She was carrying a great pile of matches in an old apron and she held one bundle in her hand as she walked. No one had brought a thing from her the whole day. ... The coaches rumbled by her. ... No one had given her a half penny; hungry and frozen, she went her way, looking so woebegone, poor little thing. ..."

The Little Flower Boy, Baltimore, 1981. Christmastime.

It was dreadfully cold. It was snowing, and the evening was beginning to darken. In the cold and the dark, the poor little boy was bareheaded. The tiny child — maybe 11, maybe 16 — was selling flowers on the busy street around the corner from his father's cart. But he was not getting any buyers because it was getting late and people were hurrying home. And they had Christmas on their minds. ...

> "Ah, a match might do some good, whoosh, it gave out
> a bright light, just like a candle. ... The little girl thought
> she was sitting in front of a great brass stove with polished
> brass knobs and fittings, the fire was burning so cheerfully
> and its warmth so comforting. ... But the fire went out and
> the stove disappeared. ..."

The little flower boy did not have on enough clothes for a cold day, so I

went up to him. And gently, I said, "How's business?" He didn't answer.
"I would like to buy some flowers." He had four bundles left.
"Five dollars apiece," he answered.
I reached in my purse and found my wallet. I opened it there in the darkening night. I put my hands on a $20 bill and a $5. I gave him the $5 and took the flowers.
But how could I leave him? It was Christmas, and I thought of the Little Match Girl, the saddest tale, so well remembered from my childhood.
I handed him my $20, with fear and trepidation that I would come off as some patronizing lady-be-bountiful.
"It's Christmas," I said.
He looked distrustful and said, "My Pa will whoop me if I have this much money."
"But tell him it's Christmas. You need some new shoes."
"He'll buy me some as soon as he gets him a job; he was laid off."
I also offered my wool scarf for his head, but he wouldn't take it, saying his Pa would think he had stolen it.
He took the $20 and, although he never exactly said, "thank you," he smiled. And that's all I needed, even though saddened by knowing he needed much, much more.
Which tells me that even though it is still more blessed to give than to receive, the needy are still of street corners.
Andersen's Little Match Girl? Well, as you know, she kept on lighting the rest of her matches and with each one she saw a vision of a happy home, of hope and comfort. With the light from her very last match, she saw her dead Granny whom she had loved. And in her vision Granny scooped her up and they went to heaven and the little girl died happy, we were told. She was found the next day frozen to death in a city doorway, but with a smile on her lips, her vision intact.
And my Little Flower Boy? I hope he, too, saw visions with my $20, visions of new shoes, a scarf, or whatever else he needed. Because beautiful visions are what Christmas is made of.

Giving a Gift from the Heart

This is a story about an 82-year-old man, a baby and a train.

Realizing that you can't take it with you, a man and his wife began taking stock of what they no longer needed.

In a small storage bin in their Florida condo, there was an old-fashioned Lionel standard-gauge train with all the tracks. Like many of us, the man had a hard time getting rid of things that reminded him of his childhood.

What could he do with his old friend? Give it to a museum? Sell it? He'd get good money for it, but he really wanted to keep it in the family.

Before he retired, he kept the train in a box in the basement of his Washington home, hoping someone would love it. The couple has three children, beautiful girls. They all are grown now with families of their own. He had hoped one of his daughters would have a boy. But none of them did.

He must have decided he didn't want to wait for the arrival of a great-grandson. Maybe he was feeling his age. Although he looks great, he readily acknowledges that he is 82.

He says a train is a very personal thing to a boy — especially to a boy raised in the cold winters of Minnesota in the days before television. The memories of long hours getting away from his sisters, playing conductor and building things around the train set in the basement are still poignant.

It seems that little boys like trains more than little girls do.

Call it gender-conditioning. My boys loved their train sets. I found the trains nothing but noisy and always in need of repair with an oil can or my sewing machine screwdriver. What's more, toy trains have the capacity for catastrophe that little boys like. "Train off the track!" was not music to this mother's ears.

On Thanksgiving, my extended family gathered in my son's Cleveland home with lots of good will and good food. It was there that the older man saw my daughter's 6-month-old son. I caught the gentleman smiling and watching the baby, no doubt remembering days long gone.

He asked my daughter, who was cradling her son, if she would like the train for Max.

Her eyes — and her husband's — brightened with expectation. How great it would be to have an authentic, old-fashioned toy train as their baby grows into boyhood.

The baby's father also knew what every male parent knows — that he would be spending time playing with the train, too.

Would it take up too much room? the older man asked. Would it be in their way? After all, it will be a few years before the baby could play with the train?

Well, the other day the train arrived in a huge box, just in time for Max's first Christmas.

As my daughter opened the box, she was touched by the meticulousness of the packaging. The train was packed in newspapers dated as far back as the 1930s. The instructions were even intact. It was as if it had never been used. But, of course, it had been used lovingly.

A letter came with the train that touched us more than the actual gift. The man didn't say "enjoy" like people say today when they give a gift.

In shaky, large script, he wrote how thrilled he was to find a boy who didn't have a train yet. He wanted Max to have as many wonderful times with the train as he had.

The train was given with love and hope. And that's what Christmas is all about — giving and remembering. In fact, of all the presents you could give at Christmas, giving someone something you own and love is probably the ultimate gift.

Undoubtedly, the train will be Max's most treasured Christmas present. The train is now assembled, and it chugs hard as it circles the baby's first Christmas tree. Max loves it when the train lights up and the whistle blows. Of course, he doesn't know what on Earth it is. But some day he will, and he will know the value of a gift given in the true spirit of Christmas.

From Far Away, to Grandmother's House they come

The grandmother had not seen her new grandchild; distances were too great, and money was too tight. But now the day had come. In a few hours, she would see her first grandbaby, who was only 32 days old.

It was Christmas Eve. The grandmother and grandfather had cleaned house at least three times in the past few days. This baby was the child of their firstborn and her husband. The arrival was more exciting than that of a royal entourage.

What is it about waiting for someone you love that makes time go by so very slowly? Life seemed so vital while waiting, yet the hands of the clock seemed to put the hours on hold.

What would she really look like? The grandmother had seen pictures. But pictures didn't tell you of the softness of the hair, the feel of the tender cheeks, the little stars that dance in a baby's eyes, the cooing noise and the smell of talcum powder at the back of the neck.

Would she cry a lot? Would their crib be all right?

The couple had allowed about an hour to get to the airport, just in case. The grandmother gave another look at the turkey and casseroles. She was ready; she had plumped the pillows on the sofa 10 times now and had stoked the fire at least six times. The Christmas tree was trimmed and the lights had been turned on hours ago. The grandfather was trying to sit and read the paper, pretending that men do not get anxious. Only the puffs coming from his pipe showed his true nervousness.

The telephone. He got it. He came into the kitchen.

"Guess what. There is kind of a storm out there. That was Sally. She called from Pittsburgh. ..."

"Pittsburgh? What are they doing in Pittsburgh?" The grandmother tried to keep her voice light.

"It seems the storm was so bad they couldn't land in Chicago, so they were sent on to Pittsburgh. But now don't worry, honey, they are just fine. The airline is putting the whole flight on a bus, and they'll be here about, well, they aren't sure, sometime in the early morning."

She turned back to the kitchen sink and looked out the window. Yes, it was starting to snow. She scrubbed the kitchen sink another time. Tears flowed down her cheeks. The grandmother was used to disappointments in her life. But she cried for her husband, too, who was sitting in front of the TV now, holding the newspaper upside down.

"They'll be just fine, don't worry," he said for the umpteenth time in their married life.

They spent the night in the front room by the fire, near the phone. They got the call to go to the bus station at 3 in the morning.

"You stay here, dear," he said. "No point in both of us going. The roads aren't too bad." So she stayed and vacuumed once more. She didn't look out the window because the snow was covering now. She prayed a little.

Finally, they came. The long night was over. As the young couple bounded through the door, snowflakes clinging to their clothes, she took the beautiful baby from their arms.

Yes, she was beautiful. She was asleep, and there were a few snowflakes on her red cheeks and a smile played on her small lips, or maybe the tears of joy in the grandmother's eyes kept her from seeing clearly. That can happen with grandmothers.

It was finally Christmas.

Chapter 12

Double,
double

Oil Trouble

Her Umbrella Complicates a Gas Station Adventure

I knew I had to tackle it eventually — the self-service gasoline station.

I also wanted to be a credit to the women's movement.

I needed the experience behind me. (As it turned out, I got it all over me.)

So on a rainy day last week, I wasted more than a few gallons of gasoline driving around trying to find a self-service station.

Finally, my target in sight, I pulled up, took a deep breath, looked to see if anyone was watching, jumped out — and then remembered I had to search for the key to my tank.

All this time, the raindrops kept falling on my head. But I didn't feel like singing.

I located the key deep in the caverns of my pocketbook and struggled to unlock the gas cap, not an easy job. It took three more rainy minutes. I got my umbrella out.

Then I moved into action, taking the hose off the hook, which is no easy trick while holding an umbrella.

Apparently, I became a little trigger happy, because before I could stick the hose into my gas tank, I had gasoline dripping over my hands, shoes and slacks.

But I loved seeing those numbers on the gas pump roll.

It gave me a real sense of power, which I've always had over my appliances at home. And now this!

But then when they stopped rolling, it wasn't so easy getting the hose out of the tank. I had to lock the tank with one hand, juggle the umbrella in the other and hold the strap of my pocketbook between my teeth.

And since there was no attendant, where do you put the money? It came to $6.

Was this one of those computer gas stations? Should I look for a slot in which to slip the bill?

Should I attach the soggy dollars to the pump with a note and a hair clip?

So I did what any self-service veteran would do. I strode knowingly up to the station and opened the door. I found a man in a chair. He looked as if he's been asleep.

He peered at me with one jaundiced eye.

"Did you make it out there, lady?"

"Just fine, thank you," I said, standing there soaked in gasoline and water, hoping he wouldn't light a cigarette.

And just to show him I knew the ropes, I said, "Here's your money, and could I have a wash rag to clean off my windshield?"

"Lady, why don't you come back later to wash your windshield — like when the rain stops?"

And he was still laughing at me when I pulled away, spinning my wheels slightly and gunning my engine.

Ms. Fixit and the Guy with
Car Trouble on the Freeway

I guess everyone has fantasies. And I'm not talking about just sexual ones, either. Believe me, there are a lot of others out there; I asked around.

Growing up, I think mine were pretty simple. For a while, I wanted to be a great opera star, not just any old opera star, but the world's greatest. Of course, I couldn't sing, but that didn't make any difference. Then I wanted to spend a night at Lincoln's feet, so to speak, at the Lincoln Memorial in Washington.

But for a long time now, I have had this fantasy I would like to share with you. It's not sexy, but it is sexist.

In the fantasy, I am stuck on an exit ramp in a traffic jam — "rolling back-ups" they call them — when the car in front of me just stops. The distress blinkers go on and the harried driver, a man, jumps out of the car, opens the hood and looks in. Then, turning to the cars now stacked up 10 deep behind him, he shrugs his shoulders.

Then I jump out of my car and run over. I'm in high heels and dressy clothes.

"Hi, can I help?" I say, and he gives me one of those "but-you-are-a-woman" stares and replies, "Well, no, hon, I don't think so. I think it's the whole darn motor."

He's a big guy and looks capable of just about anything.

But I lean under the hood and say, like a doctor, "How's your idle?"

"Bad, it's been idling real fast," he says.

I put my hand on a disconnected wire and plug it back into his distributor.

"Try the motor now, but don't step on the gas too hard, you've flooded it," I yell at him.

He looks dumbfounded, but climbs into the car and turns it over. Of course it starts, and — this is the part of the fantasy I love — he is overcome with gratitude. He gets out and shakes my hand, then kneels at my feet, and all the people in the line behind us honk and give me the victory sign before we all proceed to work.

Later, the man writes me a letter of commendation to the Hall of Fix-it Fame. Boy, I love this fantasy.

You see, all my life I've never known what's under the hood, and I've been angry that it seems to be a man's world out there in car land. Sure, there are some women grease moneys, but not enough. So part of my fantasy, I guess, is getting back at all the men who have said to me, "Hon, I can fix it if you just get back in the car. Now don't touch, or you might get hurt."

Mean, isn't it? But as fantasies go, I think it's pretty tame. Take my friend Millie. Her fantasy is that she wants to be a male rock star for just a week. Then there's Mike, who wants to hang glide under the St. Louis arch, and Sylvia, who wants to be a shepherd, and Eddie, who says he'd really like to be a bird in the San Diego Zoo.

All I want to be is a mechanic.

Our Heroine Takes
Dirty Course in Auto Repair

This is the first and second part of a story about women under the hood. Every woman should know her car. Any relation to any person living or dead, or any car known to any such person, is purely coincidental.

Every woman should. Yep, every woman should know what's under her hood, of her car, that is.

I was driving my husband's new car for the first time and had to pull into a filling station because I heard a funny noise in the motor.

I asked the young boy, "Will you look under the hood for me, please?"

He went around to the back of the car, and I yelled at him, "Listen, the noise was coming from the motor, you know, up front there."

He said, as he came back to the window, "Lady, your motor on this car is in the rear. ..." (Three men were standing by laughing.)

I jumped out of the car to defend my position, "You see, it's a new car and..." He fixed the knock. It was the jack knocking in the trunk.

I never went back to that filling station.

Then there was the day I pulled over to the side of the road because there was steam coming from the front end of the car. But I remembered I didn't know how to put up the hood. You know, it says in your driver's handbook, "put up your hood if you're in trouble and fly something white from the aerial or door handle."

Well, I had nothing white on but my undies, and I couldn't get the dern hood up no matter how much I pushed. So I just waited in the car about two hours and read road magazines and old gasoline receipts, until finally a policeman stopped and lifted up the hood and said, "It's just your radiator, cool it."

After that I said to myself, "I must learn more about you, you devil car, you." You see, I really hate the car, I think. I mean, they say love is akin to hate, and it's true. I love the inside of my car. I love the dashboard with all those shiny buttons that jump to my touch.

I love the glove compartment where I keep a flashlight, three bobbins from the sewing machine, a dog hair brush and some Johnson's baby powder. The only reason I really put up with a car is because it gets me there.

But the rest of the car I hate. It hates me, too. Like a horse, the car knows the difference between my husband and me. It burps, barks, shakes, knocks or has flat tires when I drive it, but it does nothing but purr when he gets in behind the wheel.

So what did I do? I registered at the local high school for a night course in auto mechanics. Really, girls, you should, too.

It was a fine course. There were 23 men in the class and only two women. Never had so much fun in my life. Where can you go on Wednesday night that isn't PTA or church circle where there are so many masculine-looking guys?

I joined to learn how to change a tire and how to open the hood. But I learned how to look attractive in blue jeans, smock and shatter proof glasses while relining the brakes.

We had an excellent teacher, named Jerry. He went on the premise that you should take as good care of your car as you do your body. Always replace parts that are giving you trouble, he used to say.

I just wish he'd been my physics teacher in high school. I might have passed.

It was sort of scary the first night, as he appeared in a white coat like a surgeon's, the only difference being he didn't have blood spots on his white coat, just some grease stains.

He treated every car like a very sick patient.

We saw films, dirty films. I mean, films dealing with dirty brake cylinders and dirty carburetors.

I will share with you some of the things I learned. I learned that cars have more than one dipstick; that the way a car stops, kids, isn't the way you think. (It's not like putting your foot out and braking against the wheel or the road, like in your first go-cart.)

Here's what happens: When you put your foot on the brake pedal, it compresses the fluid to the wheel cylinder, which in turn applies the brake shoes to the drum, which causes friction and stops the wheel.

We learned how to take off a wheel and get it back on. What a triumph for me.

Did you know that that thing in the center over the engine that looks like an upside-down frying pan is just an air cleaner? Did you know that there are three kinds of brakes? Under hydraulic comes: A) manual adjusting, B) self adjusting regular and C) disc.

Did you know that brakes have shoes, just like people, and spelled the same way? There are primary brake shoes and secondary brake shoes — just like when you were a kid, kind of.

Did you know that there are six or eight major hoses that run around under that hood doing things? And in some cars, there are three fan belts.

When I first looked under a hood, I almost got nauseated. Surely, the inside of a person's stomach looks better than that complicated, smelly mechanism. I think I'd rather take out a gall bladder than take out an oil filter again.

The fourth night, when I had to take off the wheel and put all those little things, like springs, rubbing points out on a white towel, so that I would get them back in the same order — no surgeon could have been any more fearful.

I know how the lady felt the night we worked on carburetors and she came in crying with her carburetor in pieces in her hands. She couldn't get it back together. I cried, too, when I tried to help her. We also learned how to check the oil: pull out that dippy dipstick! Just to show you how important it is for a woman to learn these tricks, a friend of mine, Carol Lane, who travels for a major oil company, let me in on some secrets.

She lectures and tells people how to keep up their car and shortcuts to traveling, and even how to fold a road map while driving 60 miles per hour. She said, "Those men, like your husband and mine, who jump out of the car when the service attendant looks under the hood, really don't know anything about 'under the hood.'"

They just jump out to show off or to stretch their legs or use the rest room. Since knowing Carol and having had my course, I jump out and check my oil at the filling station. Oh, how they hate me!

Oh, one more thing. You know that box-like contraption called the battery with six little caps on top?

Well, I used to see a service station man peek into just one of those caps sometimes. Did you know that it is better to peek into all of them to see the water level? So I check my own battery now. They love me to do that.

Just let me say this. My course was plenty worth it, not to the teacher maybe, as he finally had to tell me I might have to be a "repeater," if I wanted the course for credit.

A sad thing happened to me. On or about my sixth lesson, I had to drop out. Jerry said, "You must bring a car to class, so you can get practical experience. ..."

I told my husband, on a Tuesday night, I remember because it was snowing. "Honey, I have to have a car. ..."

"For show and tell?" he asked.

"Not exactly. It's for homework. We have to take it apart sort of, you know. ..."

There was a lengthy exchange of gunfire, I mean rapid-fire talk, and the next day I had to tell the teacher that my husband didn't want me tampering with his car parts. And do you know no one in that class would share his or her car with me, even the old lady with the 1934 Chevy!

Chapter 13

Snakes and
Snails and
Fairy Tails

Brothers Grimm Wove Grim Tales

Believe it or not, at naptime the other day the grandchildren let me pick the book we'd read. Good. I had read "The Cat In The Hat" for the 400th time, and I always fell asleep before they did, due to the monotonous drone of my own voice.

I got out my copy of "Grimms' Fairy Tales." And wow, they are really grim. In fact, they contain nearly as many criminal or kinky acts as today's violence-prone television lineup or movie offerings.

Did you know that the Grimm brothers were fresh out of law school when they started their collection? Did you know that they took the words just from hearsay and fourth-hand from local townsfolk? No accuracy there.

In the foreword of the book, it says don't be worried about the cruel things that happen in the stories, because they happen to the bad people. I disagree. Sometimes they happened to the goodies.

I mean, take Hansel and Gretel — you have to, the mom and pop didn't want them. They were abandoned in the woods. Their parents said, "Listen, kids, we're too poor to feed you. You'll have to go." (No welfare checks there.)

A case of child abuse?

When they got lost, they came to a gingerbread home, decorated with candies, and they started nibbling, literally eating the house up. A case of invasion of privacy or illegal entry?

But the old witch who lived there gets hold of the kids, and tries to fatten them up in order to eat them.

Premeditated murder or revenge?

Think what a modern DA would do with those kids, or the witch, for that matter? I mean, who was in the right?

Through trickery Gretel finds a way to push the wicked witch into her own oven. Ugh!

Then Hansel and Gretel really loot her house of the precious jewels and make off with them. Robbery?

How did those kids know the witch was going to turn on the oven switch and bake Hansel? Maybe she was just kidding around. Did they fry her in the end? The story never makes this clear.

Also what about Rumpelstiltskin? Where a poor miller bragged to a king that his beautiful daughter could spin gold out of straw. Downright lying.

The king made the girl a queen, but locked her in the castle room with a spinning wheel and said, "Go to it." Remember?

Then a little man came to her and bribed her time and time again. Saying things like "I'll spin the straw into gold if you will give me your first-born."

But the poor queen had to guess this little old man's name on the last demand. A case of out-and-out extortion.

Meantime, the queen had sent a messenger into the woods who was an undercover agent, a kind of early-day plumber or stoolie, and the spy found out the little old man's name.

Then the climax of the story. When the queen told the little old extortionist his real name, he got so mad he split himself in two.

Do you know anyone that has done that lately? What a way to go. What violence.

I mean, one thing about the "Cat In The Hat:" I'd rather fall asleep reading a children's book than shudder.

Today's Cinderella
Can Stay Out Past Midnight

Once upon a time, but not so long ago, there was a beautiful young girl who lived with her widowed stepmother and two mean stepsisters.

She was called "Cinderella" because she had to do all the housework and especially clean the cinders from the hearth. They lived in the country and used wood to heat their small house.

The stepsisters were always mean to Cinderella. They were jealous because she was so much prettier than they were. Sometimes they hit Cinderella. Sometimes they hit their own mother, and sometimes the stepmother hit her own children.

But Cinderella had no other place to live, so she would just do her work and sit by the fire in the winter. And she would play in the woods nearby in the summer with her forest friends. And sometimes she would read late into the night. She was lonely.

She went to school, but she didn't have many friends because she could never have them over to play. Then, too, there was another problem: The stepmother was very old and feeble. So Cinderella was afraid that the mean sisters would hurt their own mother. Sometimes they forgot to feed her. So Cinderella fixed all the elderly woman's meals. Also, the sisters were plotting to put their own mother in a nursing home.

Now, one fine day word came out that the mayor of the town was having a great ball. He sent out fancy invitations. But the wicked stepmother said, "Cinderella, you can't go." And, in truth, Cinderella didn't think it possible that she could go. She didn't have a ball gown, and she didn't have nice shoes. The ugly sisters started preparing for the ball, but Cinderella knew she had to stay home and keep her stepmother.

The night of this great ball came. And Cinderella sat by the fire and dreamed. If only she could go to the ball. Maybe she could meet a handsome young man, and he would fall in love with her.

Suddenly, there was a fairy godmother in front of her. And she said, "Cinderella, with this magic wand I can transform your house dress into a beautiful ball gown and you can go to the ball. I will turn one of those pumpkins out there into a golden carriage, and I will transform the dirty rats in the attic into coachmen."

"Yes, I would like to go to the ball. But don't bother about a pumpkin or a carriage, I would not know how to drive either. Can you transport me there on a magic carpet? I don't even need to have a ball gown. I like this dress. It is new. I just made it myself out of some old flour sacks. And I wouldn't need new shoes. I could go barefoot — the night is warm. But you will have to get a baby-sitter for my stepmother."

Of course, she thought she was dreaming. And the nice fairy godmother didn't tell her she had to be home by midnight, like in the old days, you know, things being what they are today.

So you know the story, only the ending is a little different. When the fairy waved her small wand, Cinderella saw a brand new yellow car out front, with a driver. Or was it a taxicab? But no fancy carriage. The pumpkins weren't really ripe yet. She hurriedly cleaned up. She fixed her beautiful hair and put it on top of her head, which made her look older. And she noticed the godmother had changed one of the rats into a nice sitter. She jumped into the waiting car, and off they went to the ball.

At the big dance, she met the mayor's son, who was very handsome. He was a lawyer and the best in the town, a real catch. And guess what? He had eyes only for this beautiful girl in her plain cotton dress and bare feet. They fell in love. And six months later, they were married.

Meantime, the mayor's son, who was a very kind man, asked the stepmother to come live with them in their new house. She did, and from then on the stepmother changed her ways because she was much happier. She was almost loving to her stepdaughter. And Cinderella and her fella begged the sisters to have some counseling. But they rejected that idea. They continued to fight.

Cinderella and her fine husband, who were trying very hard to live happily ever after, tried to explain to the sisters that they, too, could be happier and prettier if they tried to be nicer to one another and other people.

But no one knows to this day whether those two sisters ever found happiness or husbands.

Which all goes to show you that you don't always have to have fine clothes to go to a ball. And that love can change things. But that change is still hard to come by. But we can keep on trying.

Little Red Riding Hood on Mean Streets

Once upon a time, but not so long ago, there was a little girl named Little Red Riding Hood. She was called that because her mother had made her a nice goose-down red jacket with a hood (as the winter was very cold).

Little Red Riding Hood and her mother didn't have a lot of money, because her father left home when she was a baby. So her mother worked at a disco on Saturday nights to support them. The little girl didn't have a lot of clothes like the other girls. So this made her love the new jacket even more. Little Red Riding Hood had just turned 13.

One sunny day, Little Red Riding Hood's mother said to her, "Little Red Riding Hood, your grandmother is ill. Will you take this hot chicken soup in the Thermos and this pint of whiskey to her? I have to listen to 'Dialing for Millions.'"

. "Oh, Mama, I wanted to listen to a rock special this afternoon."

Now, LRRH was usually a sweet girl, but she did not always like to do chores and errands for her mother.

"Well, dear, take your radio with you, and here's the other stuff. And take this little pepper spray. If anyone bothers you, just run this button and push down and let 'em have it. It's non-lethal, but will blind someone temporarily. Now do be careful, dear, and don't talk to anyone on the way to grandmother's house."

So LRRH started out. Her grandmother lived about 20 blocks away, and she hated the long walk, but she loved her grandmother. She took off her bright red hood and let her curls bounce as she skipped joyfully along.

Suddenly out of the city park nearby came this big, bad wolf. He sauntered up, baring his sharp teeth.

"Hi ya, cutie. What cute blond curls you have. ... Where ya headed?"

"Buzz off, twerp," she said, a little too flippantly. "I'm going to my grandmother's; she is sick. And she is a black belt, so she could whomp you."

LRRH was sort of scared, but she had her spray gizmo that she could use in an emergency.

She walked on smiling, listening to WOFM-ROCK and pausing here and there to talk to a pigeon or a thin city squirrel.

The wolf followed her, but she did not see him. She got to her grandmother's house and knocked on the door. Her grandmother had to get out of her sickbed to unlock the dead bolt and the three other locks.

She told her grandmother about the scary wolf.

"Pour some soup out for us, dearie, and leave some there by the door in case the bad wolf tries to get in. Also, never fear, I am armed if anyone comes on my property."

Now, right here, I bet you are thinking there aren't real wolves anymore who frighten or hurt people. Well, in this story there is.

And sure enough, there was a rap at the door and a voice said, "Meter man, may I come in?"

Would you believe the grandmother forgot to look out her window? She opened all the locks to let the "meter man" in. It was the big, bad wolf.

LRRH's grandmother threw the soup in the wolf's face and wrestled him to the ground. It was true; she was a black belt. Then she tied him to the heavy oak dining-room table. "Call the police," she told LRRH.

Chapter 14

Summer Son

The Borrowers of Summer

Shakespeare said it well. "Neither a borrower nor a lender be. ..." Of course, he didn't have a bunch of neat things like a blender with 10 speeds that made great frozen daiquiris or a vacuum that had a waxing attachment or a microwave oven. Right?

I've found that summer brings out the borrower like the bees.

There are four classes of borrowers:

Class A: the type who borrows your tennis racket, breaks three strings and buys you a new one that's better than the one you had. This borrower rates an "X" for excellent.

Class B: the type who borrows your hedge clippers, brings them back, smiling all the while, thanking you very much, and two weeks later you find out they don't work. Rate this one "PR" for poor risk.

Class C: the type who never brought back your electric popcorn popper, and when you asked for it six months later, says, "Who, me? I've never seen your popper. I once borrowed John Doe's. As a matter of fact, we don't even like popcorn a whole lot." Yet you know he has it. Rate this one "B" for bad.

Class D: the type who asks to borrow a half-cup of pickle juice, and let me tell you, you never see the pickle juice again. Chalk it up to a "grant," not a loan. And say to yourself who needs pickle juice anyway? Rated "G" for gone.

Here are just a few things I've loaned out this summer and never expect back: snorkel equipment, a goldfish bowl, a hoe, a glove stretcher, an ice bag, a baby car seat and a sump pump.

But that's OK, these items may be my penance for my "over-borrowing" at times.

My confession. Here are the things I've borrowed over the last 10 years but have taken back. A soup kettle, a carpet needle, a playpen, hair clippers and one dog for the night when mine was at the vet's while my husband was out of town.

But this summer I have borrowed and have not taken back: eight books, two cups of mayonnaise, one sprig of parley, one pimento, one stalk of celery, one cup of distilled water and one bag of kitty litter.

So my slate is not lily white.

Summer rules: Know your borrower. Is she neat, clean and a good housekeeper? Or are her kitchen, top bureau drawer and her fingernails in the same messy category? If she's messy, you will never see the item again.

There are two ways to handle a constant borrower. Just say, "no," and she'll never speak to you again. Or say "yes," and borrow from her the most expensive thing she has: her car, her piano, her color TV or her Oscar de la Renta dress. And she'll never speak to you again.

So for those of you out there I've borrowed from, rest assured I will return these items as soon as this column hits the street.

Oh yes, Virginia, I have not forgotten about the time you loaned me your husband for a whole evening to fix my thermostat. I'll pay you back, I promise.

Summertime Travel Takes a Severe Toll

What has four wheels and flies? No, not your garbage truck. Your car with your husband behind the wheel on a trip to the beach.

For those of you who are going on a short car vacation, I feel for you. Why is it the man of the household drives faster on a family car trip than he does when he is escorting you to a dinner party?

Simple, dearie. There are four children, one dog, coloring books, melting crayons, paper dolls, soft drinks, spilled popcorn and sandwiches sprawled out in the car with him. He is simply not used to being confined in a compact space with the kids and you and all those props.

So he drives faster to get there sooner. Get it? The sooner he gets to the beach, the sooner he can get out of the car, release his pent-up emotions and pretend he is single.

Some of our worst marital discords have come about in the "vacation-mobile," alias family car. Sample:

Him: Will you ever learn to fold a road map correctly? I can't see the highway if you don't fold it up right.

Me: When you empty your pipe out the window, the ashes fly back on the children in the back seat. And are you going to ask me to drive when we go through the cities like you usually do?

Him : Ask all the kids to take off their shoes. Someone is kicking the back of my seat. And who has an inner tube that's leaking air?

Me : All the children are barefoot since the air conditioner broke down, remember? And you almost broke the tollgate barrier. Could you slow down for those?

Him : I hate toll gates, detours and dirt roads. Didn't you know that tomatoes always get watery in sandwiches? Couldn't you have used ham?

Me : Ham makes us all more thirsty and then we have to drink more and then we have to go.

Him: I'll make three potty stops a day. That ought to be enough. Are the kids dressed nice enough to go into that restaurant up ahead?

Me : Yes, but I'm not. I just spilled Coke on my white shorts.

Him : Then we'll have to fast-food it again.

Me : So what else is new? Did you lock the garage door?

Him : No, for heavens sake, I told you to. Didn't you? I think I left my fingernail clippers at home.

Me : Whatever we do, let's not go back. I couldn't stand the extra miles.

Him : Why does this trip seem longer each summer?

Me : Because you get older each summer.

The Dark Side of the
Annual Vacation at the Shore

The first thing we noticed about the house was a list of dos and don'ts posted on the fridge, kind of a boot-camp directive. Instead of "Welcome to Casa del Smith" we read:

"Indoor barbecue does not work, don't light it; do not flush toilet while someone is taking a shower; keep screen doors closed at all times; don't pull shades down; don't use kitchen exhaust fan, it is broken; prop chair against oven door if you want to close it; don't take baths on weekends; water pressure is low; don't let sand accumulate on the stairs; don't dance on deck" and a few more cautions.

But these were just the primary no-nos. Once moved in, we found a bathtub that didn't drain, mattresses that slipped off the beds, spiders that wouldn't get out of bed and mosquitoes that never stopped biting.

It's funny, but in the winter when the snow is falling, all of us dream of beautiful beaches or the mountains, somewhere, anywhere, where nature takes precedence over technology. I guess it's called wanderlust or vacation or bust. So we booked this beach house by phone. It had been billed as "a wonderful four-bedroom home overlooking the sea."

Uh-huh. The only view of the sea turned out to be through a tiny bathroom porthole, and the ocean was two blocks away.

And although I brought sheets, towels, jars of peanut butter, jelly, canned hams, paper plates, toilet paper, plastic forks and spoons, a can opener and clothes, what we really needed I didn't bring.

We needed antihistimine for our mosquito bites, lots of alcohol for the fly bites (plus some to drink), a heavy sunscreen, a bathing suit that stayed on after being struck by a wave, a board for my squishy bed, an electric fan and bottled water.

I'd also forgotten about what happens when a big family that stays together sleeps together. With the walls of paper, if anyone snored or clipped his toenails, it woke up everyone. I'd forgotten about the sand between my sheets after three children had been playing cards on my bed. I'd forgotten about how sand feels in your teeth.

Some little one took the labels off the canned goods, but it didn't matter, because we had to eat out due to the bad water pressure.

Looking back now, as I sit at my office, with my desk piled with mail, I think the important thing to take to the beach is money — money to eat out at every good restaurant, money to play miniature golf, money to buy rafts, umbrellas and boat trips, money to buy your way up and down the boardwalk on a rainy day.

However, I must say that on about the fourth day of various complaints, I made a speech, because we are spoiled, of course. I wanted to tell the children about the old days, when there was no television and air conditioning.

So I said, "Look kids, we wait all year to be at the beach. Now, just pretend you're camping out. If you can't take a bath, just go dip in the ocean. Think of the ancient tribesmen. When they were here, they didn't have all the luxuries when they lived by the sea."

But some smarty piped up and said, "Yeah, mom, but they weren't paying hundreds of dollars for a yucky beach home, either."

But you know what? We'll be back next year. Because the ocean is the ocean and it remains the same. Magnificent.

Home is Hilton for Freeloaders

One of the most active games we play at our house in the summer is called "musical beds."

It's the penalty one pays for living in a resort or historical area or near a big state park. In other words, if you lived in Muleshoe, Okla., where no one visits for long, you don't have to worry about this game.

This summer, not only were all our beds always taken, but I changed sheets at least 100 times. Sofa cushions, roll-aways and patio chaises were put into use for visitors. I moved kids from bed to floor and floor to bed faster than you can say, "Howdy."

In summer, our house is the Freeloader's Hilton, even with the room service nil.

Don't misunderstand me. I love company. That is when they come to visit with fewer than 2 1/2 children, no pets, a car that is in good working order, a high chair, a playpen, paper diapers, paper plates and cups, a few groceries and, hopefully, an extra sleeping bag.

It's amazing how close and friendly some fourth cousins become if you live near the water. Sometimes the letter announcing their arrival "arrives" the same day they arrive. Which means you have no time to write and tell them your kids have any number of contagious diseases.

There was Cousin Joe with his six kids and new wife, who had never seen the Washington Monument. There was Aunt Effie, whom we hadn't seen in 20 years, and her 84-year-old companion, who was on a soy bean and sea-weed diet.

There was Myrt and Jim, who brought two bed-wetting children, their pet raccoon and an alarm clock that went off at 5:30 every morning.

The Johnsons are "coming by" next week, and my husband just said, "Call and see how much it would cost us to spend the night in that motel up the pike with the lighted swimming pool and closed-circuit TV. And be sure you get the Johnsons' address and directions to their summer home in the Poconos before they leave our house."

Summer camp:
The Kids Have Never Had It So Good

My friends, the Smiths, have just sent their three kids off to summer camp. Before the youngsters left, however, their parents received an amazing booklet, sort of a cross between novitiate rules, boot camp regulations and a retirement home brochure.

When my mother sent me to camp, she mailed a check, put name tags on all my clothes, kissed me goodbye and said, "See you in six weeks."

Not nowadays. The Smiths' brochure read like a shiny college handbook. It must have been written by one of the psych majors who is a counselor at the camp.

First, they ask you to write you camper every day. I never wrote my kids at camp for fear they would get homesick.

And, the booklet advises, make "no phone calls unless they are an emergency and then they must be joint ones to the director and the young camper." Wow, talk about early censorship. And what constitutes an emergency with a child? Poison ivy or a bunkmate who puts frogs in your bed every night? It also says, "If a phone call is made by your camper, do not become hysterical at the sound of a teardrop on the receiver."

My camp didn't even have a phone. Besides, my mother would never have heard a teardrop on a receiver. She was too busy yelling at my brothers and sisters and swatting mosquitoes.

Of course, I do remember running away from camp with my cousin. We were homesick, but didn't get two miles down the mountain. You see, we discovered a boys' camp nearby. We learned to love camp.

Here's what today's camp brochure says about homesickness: "All

campers can get over it. Like any other illness, it must be treated properly
and promptly for an immediate cure. ... Don't tell a homesick camper how
much you miss him/her or how lonesome the dog is without him/her. Tell
him/her the neighborhood is boring and all of the kids are away. That the
weather is hot and how lucky they are to be in the mountains."

But what if a kid lives in the mountains, where it's cool all summer? And
lots of kids belong to swimming clubs where you can have more fun than at
camp. My friend Mike lived next to a fire hydrant that we turned on every
day to beat the heat.

Maybe it would be better to just say: "The town you live in has gone
somewhere else, along with all the tennis courts, pools and fast-food joints.
Your mom and dad are moving to an African rain forest and taking your dog
and cat with them." That way the kids would never want to come home.

Of course, the booklet had many necessary rules about clothes and programs. But one of them poses a real hardship.

Although there is a camp store, campers are asked to deposit all money in
the camp store at the beginning of the season, and the recommended deposit
is only $7. Purchases of refreshment, postage, stationery and so forth are
charged to that account.

Now hold on, Camp Minniehaha, the ha ha is on you. I don't know any
red-blooded kid today who can exist on just $7 a week for candy, chewing
gum, video game quarters, swimming goggles, curlers, french fries,
Twinkies, Cokes, Clearasil or smuggled lipstick.

My camp, of course, didn't have a camp store, which is why my mother
sent me there in the first place.

Well, anyway, the Smith kids have been at camp a week now, and the only
thing their parents worry about is that there may be some thunderstorms. All
three of the kids wet their beds if there is a bad storm in the night.

Camping has changed, but kids haven't.

For Some, Vacation
Time Isn't Over; It Never Began

Ah, the last weekend of the summer! I'm on the beach stretched out on my now-faded towel, savoring the smell of the sand and sea. I am catching the last golden rays of sun and listening to the crying of the gulls.

The people near me on the next little island of beach towels and chairs are talking loudly. They are also drinking.

I am trying to sleep. I would like to sleep my way through the dismal winter and come out on the sunny side of next summer.

I overhear bits of what they are saying. I don't want to. There are four women, middle-aged, and one man:

"I think I will start cleaning my own house. The long trip to go get Emma and the bus fare are all, well, not really worth it. ..."

"I know what you mean. I may let the maid and the gardener go. They just aren't any good anymore. ...You know what I find appalling is that there is all this unemployment and yet you can't get anyone to cook or clean. ..."

"Have you learned to cook yet, Flo? We have such a good cook, but she won't do any cleaning and she won't make beds. ..."

"I will tell you one thing. I wouldn't have a maid that won't make beds. ... Our house is so big, do you realize that I have five bathrooms?"

Suddenly, I can't stand the noise from Elitedom. I pick up my towel, my paperback, my sunscreen and my thongs and walk back up the beach.

I find a spot and I lie down and let my eyes and ears take in the last view of the ocean and the sweet sounds.

Now I am restless. My mind has been triggered. I think of the little row-house in the inner city I pass every day. Two women and a little girl perch on the steps in shorts and bare feet, clutching cans of frosty soda pop. I wonder if they are there right now? Have they got a fan for the inside? Do they have enough soda pop for the hot weekend? It is still very hot in the city.

Sometimes, sitting in my car waiting for the light to change, I can hear them talking.

Today, they're probably talking about the high cost of buying school supplies, because in just a few days the little girl will be going back to school. I am hoping they have the money for her lunch box and a new dress.

And I realize that Flo's bathing suit would pay for three dresses and a new lunch box.

Then the pounding of the encroaching ocean drowns out my ruminations on life's disparities.

I start to run up the beach. Maybe it is time for summer to come to an end. Because for many people, summer doesn't mean vacation time. For some, summer is just another passage of time to struggle through.

The Last of the Roses

Much has been written about the last rose of summer, I know.

But just one more time, bear with me. I would like to tell you about the rose, the last one, perhaps, in our small garden.

I am standing surrounded by early-morning dew, now called frost. I am dressed for work, but something about the sunrise lures me out here to look around with longing and observe the last vestiges of what was a profusion of summer blooms. After all, there won't be too many times that I will get to do this before winter grabs my garden.

My husband loves roses. He is actually the gardener. He knows how to tend and take care of them. I pick them, admire them and talk to them when no one is around.

But he knows their real names.

It's late October, and I'm feeling slightly saddened by the end of another summer. Warm, sometimes too hot, but an outdoor time, vacation time, a time of dogs barking, of lawn mowers roaring, of children on skateboards, cries and laughter that spread like crabgrass across neighborhood yards.

I have picked the only rose in bloom this morning, a deep crimson, a bud that I hope will open and add one last touch of real perfume in our house.

I hate picking it as it is such a noble thing, and it is carrying on as best it can against the ravages of fall. I don't have to use the scissors. Its stem is already weakened — it had been forewarned of winter — and the thorns are even softer.

This deep red rose, like red velvet, is named "Mr. Lincoln."

And Mr. Lincoln won't last long in the house this time of year.

I hold it and realize I hate the thought of winter's descent. I sit on a tree stump, rose in my hand, and feel a terrible sadness, a pall, a dread — I hate endings.

But suddenly I see it, the euonymus bush nearby. It is sometimes called "The Burning Bush" because it is so very scarlet, as if on fire. It will carry on the red October — new beginnings.

That is, until fall drops its mantle and the snows take over.

It's as if this burning bush knows the benefit of rejuvenation for those of us who have seen many autumns. It is assuring us that it will assume the glory in the garden.

Even so, the flower of the rose will go, but the stem work, the life force, will last, and the cycle will rotate once again.

I am suddenly elated as I realize that nature gives us this change of seasons, Earth's surprises. I guess I needed a reminder of the cyclical process.

No apocalypse here, just the triumph of The Force at its best.

When the news is all bad, when our world seems heavy with threats and disaster, there is hope to be seen in nature's intricacies.

Looking at the rose in my hand now, I no longer see just one tired flower. As my vision widens, I see that the copper mums are about to come into bloom — more continuity.

My eyes come back to the red, red, red of the euonymus bush, which now, as the sunlight hits it, is indeed fiery and sending me a message, and I will learn to be more patient.

I take the rose inside as if I am carrying a chalice, place it in a bud vase and put it, oh, so gently, on the dining room table.

An Argument for All Seasons

She's come out of the closet: She wants everyone to know she hates summer. With a passion.

She has always hated summer, but she doesn't want to make our lives miserable complaining as we sit comfortable in air conditioning.

She comes into the office and tells me, "I have to talk about it — I hate summer. I hate the heat, first. I hate the flowers, because you have to weed the flower beds. I hate the grass because you have to mow it.

"I hate the disorder of summer: children — some I don't even know — running through the house, flies coming in with the kids. I hate bee bites and frisking the kids and dogs for ticks and the general feeling of casualness. Summer is dangerous.

"I hate summer clothes. They have to be ironed and they get more wrinkled. I can't wait until I wear my first wool sweater. I hate the way people's tempers are shorter, and I hate trying to get the lawn mower or the grill started. I hate trying to think of things to cook that don't heat up the kitchen and the house. Summer foods are not easy to prepare. Don't let those ads for summer soups fool you — you have to cook them first. You can't eat the corn off the vine, and most meats have to be cooked."

On and on it went, a litany of invective trashing summer.

She seems to feel much better now that she has bared her soul and her teeth on summer's inadequacies.

I've always known this about her — she is a winter person.

In August, she starts leafing through catalogs and ordering winter clothes. She simply blooms in winter. She was born in October, which may or may not have something to do with it.

We have long conversations about the weather because I am a summer person, love summer and hate winter.

I love the warmth, the sunlight, the beach, the ocean, the crowded swimming pools and most of all, the abundance of flowers. I like the noise of my neighbors' lawn mowers. I even like the smell of sweat and bug repellent and the melodious noise of the tree toads at night. I like the long evenings and sitting outside and the squealing of kids running up and down the block.

So I suggest she move to Alaska, Norway or Iceland. She tells me to bug off and go to Florida, where it is forever summer.

She reminds me that, contrary to popular belief, statistics prove people live longer in New England than in Florida.

I tell her, "Look, in the summer you don't have to worry about snow, ice, slipping on it, shoveling it, being stranded in or on it."

"But I like being snowbound. It's beautiful and quieting. Snow beats poison ivy and too much sunburn," she says.

"Well," I haggle on, "look, have patience. I just heard a cold front is expected tonight."

"What?" she yells. "Going from 95 degrees to 85! That's a cold front?"

Then we both concede that if you wait long enough here in Baltimore or Dallas or Peoria — in 20 minutes the weather will change.

Then we both agree on one thing — where weather is concerned, there's no utopia.

So today there is a stationary cold front bringing the temperature to 75 degrees. She comes to work in a jacket, long-sleeved shirt and corduroy skirt, all new. She's smiling smugly.

She sits down to work, buttons her jacket around her while I throw off my hot canvas shoes, wiggle my toes and think iced tea.

She'd better not show up in a turtleneck and boots. "Don't push me," I warn her.

September is here, and you know, it can be hot as heck in September, thank goodness.

Fine Memories, Lifelong Friends

These two old friends meet only once a year.

My husband's best and closest buddy flies across the country to see us every July. And even though I did not grow up with them, I take part in the reunion and sit in on some of their reminiscing.

Our friend loves to be here in the summer, when Maryland is at its best — hot, yes, but lush with color and vegetation and ripe for sightseeing.

In some ways, the two men — now in their 70s — hang out together the way teen-agers do, rapping and trading thoughts.

They have known each other since they were 5-years-old. They revel in their intimate frame of reference; neither has to go back and explain anything to the other.

Having once had high-pressure "business" jobs, they are now in retirement and, coincidentally, both have become artists.

On the first day of the week's visit, they catch up on present happenings. Then they sort of reverse and go back to Texas in the 1930s to 1940s: the girlfriends they knew, the games they played, the cars they drove, their schools and teachers, the mothers they loved. They skip World War II because it is too painful — they try to keep their special time upbeat.

They also skip the operations they've had. Those dark moments are behind them, and, for now, their health is holding.

Sometimes during the week, the three of us feel like a dance trio. We are graceful, still in sync as we ruminate and recollect. We sit now and enjoy the garden in bloom: roses, gladiola, impatiens and the wonderful perfume of freshly cut grass.

As older people, we are more cerebral than kinetic. We don't sleep as long as we used to, so there seems more time for contemplation. We have trouble with food that is too hot and spicy, and although our minds are still sharp on long-term memory, we sometimes forget where we placed our sunglasses.

The two men get up at dawn and sit on the deck. I can hear their voices from my bedroom window.

I look down at them and smile, because I know they need this time to talk about the things they once did together.

I get up later and join them for breakfast.

Two handsome guys, still. A few gray hairs and few wrinkles. I like the way they cross their legs and then stretch them out when they have a good joke or have to search the past. I like to see their heads roll back as they laugh about some story from their younger days.

By the second day, they have gone from the past — teachers they hated, homemade go-carts they loved — to the present, everything from President Bush to Iran and the S&L bailouts.

And after about three days, when they've hashed over the past and the present, wrung it out like a dish rag and hung it to dry in the back of their minds, they talk of the future: what they'd do about violence, drugs, the economy and then they soar from projections on environment to the children of tomorrow.

During the summer visit, the three of us spend a lot of time planning where we'll go, which museum, which exhibit — the National Aquarium, of course, and a boat ride around the bay.

We talk about the restaurants we'll hit, and yet we know, as we've found out on other summer visits, we will get only half the things done we have planned.

What a wonderful time this is for these two — especially so because I have always maintained it is more difficult for men to establish lifelong friendships than for women.

They are like brothers, but maybe it is better that they are not related, because there is no sibling rivalry. It doesn't matter who used to get more allowance or who has a better car today.

It just matters that they have had so many past connections. And now, as those years become compressed into moments, they seem more evanescent, and so much more precious.

Following in the Footsteps

In the wet sand of early morning, no two sets of footprints look alike.

The appearance of the human foot is a marvel of ambiguity. I become entranced with it while walking at low tide during five vacation days at South Bethany Beach, Del.

Here, where the foam of the waves leaves the sand slightly vulnerable, I walk my three miles each morning.

I gaze seaward and wonder at the rhythm of the tide, the continuous reminder of nature's forces.

The first morning, like a forensic expert, a police detective, I begin to study the foot patterns in the sand — all so varied.

It becomes a challenge, a game to see if I can tell the runner from the walker, the women from the men, the overweights from the thins.

I can, and so can you.

Here the runner's foot digs deeper into the sand at the toe while the walker's foot digs in at the heel.

The male stride is longer, and the man's footprint seems to splay outward more than the woman's.

The more serious runners leave prints of designer shoes: Reebok, Nike and Adidas — wonderful designs like a modern abstract — herringbone, corrugated, geometric patterns leaving the imprint of the latest art in man's material engineering.

Even prints of the gulls give me a feeling of being part of the order of things. Their tiny imprints mingle with the record of the designer shoes.

If you get up at dawn and run or walk in the cool of the seaside morning, you are probably serious about your body: your blood pressure, your cholesterol, your weight, your muscles. These prints tell me these people are here for good health.

I try to put my footprints in some of the designs — impossible, it doesn't work. Some people seem to run incorrectly.

You may ask me now why I'm looking down at the footprints and not enjoying the magnificence of the ocean. But I am; it's never better than in the morning before the desecrators of beaches stake out a place for their noisy radios, kids, plastic throw-aways and garbage. But the footprints make me think about the human being to whom they are connected and the wonderful mechanism of the human body that works so intricately while running or walking. I ponder and praise the amazing structure presented on the sand.

Unknown footprints are as mesmerizing as the mysteries of the ocean.

I wonder about the people whose prints I study. Are they good or bad? Greedy, giving, caring, spiritual, sexual, tragic or troubled? Are they housewives, stockbrokers, truck drivers or biochemists?

Now there's a small, shoeless print: a child running with a parent. I follow their paths to a sandy knoll where they seem to have set down and rested.

I imagine them looking seaward and the child asking the same questions my 3-year-old asked when she first saw the ocean, "Mom, what makes the waves? Do they ever stop?"

I like to think about parent and child communicating without the television and the noises of home.

I was sure I'd see more men's prints than women's. Don't more men than women run in the morning?

I counted, and I found more women's — good! Things are changing.

Footprints in the sand are like dreams, ephemeral; you can read into them anything you like.

Now it's later, and the tide is encroaching on my detective work.

What fun it has been to guess about people. And as the waves start slapping at my feet, I'd like to think that these are happy people who have walked before me — as free-spirited as the soaring and ever-present gulls.

And that's what vacations are all about — doing something you don't do at work, giving space to speculation and wonderment. Unencumbered.

So Privileged, and So Bored

Their mother asks if they want to go outside and see the garden or go find the cats.

Twenty minutes later, I asked if they want a Diet Coke and some home-made brownies.

Thirty minutes later, she asks if they would like to go to the mall earlier than planned.

I ask if they want to watch television. I have a few good videos they might like.

Ten minutes later, their mother tells them, "We'll go to the Gap, I promise."

The objects of our inquiries are two teen-age girls, 12 and 14, who are on a summer trip with their mother. They had stopped by for a visit with me.

Their mother and I are old friends who had not seen each other for 10 years.

Every time we ask the girls what they want to do or suggest something to do, they say, "No, thanks," or they just shrug and roll their eyes. But, in general, they sit on the sofa and look out into space in that special vacuous way that only teen-agers can manage when they want to tune out.

Finally, the mother turns to me and says, "I know they're bored with our talk, but I will take them to the mall later. ... It's such a hard age, so sulky, and they get bored easily. At least they aren't on drugs."

Yes, I guess they were bored. They have a swimming pool at home, a VCR, home computers, their own phones and all the frills to make life full and happy.

They answered all our suggestions with glazed sighs, and they never smiled. I kind of envied their ability to turn us off so completely.

After we said goodbye, I sat wondering about life at that age.

I remember being taken in the summer to see out-of-town aunts and uncles or my parents' friends, and having to sit on a porch swing with my brother in hot weather. But no one ever asked us if we were bored. If we had a deck of cards or a book, we were fine. We laughed, we talked and we had fun.

Summer was never boring for us, but then, I'm talking the 1930s. We had no television, and radio was a nighttime thing. There were no computers, of course, but I remember having fun. I guess we knew how to do "nothing" very well.

So now I worry. Why are two middle-class kids who seem to have everything, including caring parents, suffering from what looks like terminal boredom?

I'll tell you why. They have too much. There are too many choices.

That may be an old grind, and yet, why did the mother perpetuate their feelings with "I'm sorry you're so bored. ..."

If my friend does not have access to a theme park or summer camp, will she spend the summer trying to keep her kids from boredom? Yes, and if she says it enough — "I'm sorry you're so bored" — then boredom will become a parent-induced behavior.

Time hangs heavy in the summer, and I think kids should be given something constructive to do. The mall can't substitute for life.

Yet a 14-year-old said to me yesterday: "I'm looking for a job at the mall, I don't want to baby-sit again this summer. It's so boring."

I was curious. "What would you do if you had a choice?"

"Hang glide in the Rockies," she told me.

I think that's it; they want excitement, a high.

I guess my brother and I wanted excitement too, but we knew we had to make our own.

I wonder if there's any way to tell that age that life gets exciting later on. These summer days may be the most carefree times of their lives, so they should enjoy it while they are cared for, and smile.

I always thought boredom is in the soul of the bored, but now I think it can be conveyed by parents who see it as their fault.

And, of course, tell you that truth, it is the parent's fault.

Too much too soon leads to too bored!

The Beach and the Kids

I'd forgotten what it's like to take small children to the beach. Ah, the joys. But there are nuisances.

- How a 6-year-old, who can hear a Coke bottle open from the kitchen when he's taking his nap, can't hear you yell, "It's time to come out of the ocean now."
- How kids, who won't eat a gourmet casserole or expensive roast beef at home, can consume four soda pops, six slices of pizza and two bags of french fries in a two-hour period at the beach.
- How a 9-year old who can make mud pies and wade in a rainfilled gutter back home won't sit down a the beach because of the sand in the bottom of her bathing suit.
- How a few grains of sand swell when eaten with your french fries.
- How difficult it is to get your wet bathing suit back on for the second time over your sunburned body.
- How life guards watch the pretty girls who are swimming out too far but don't see the 3-year-old who is trying to drown his brother at the ocean's edge.
- How inconsiderate people bring their transistor radios onto the beach, lie down near you, but won't turn on YOUR station.
- How many hands of Old Maid you can play in one day, inside the apartment while watching the rain pelt the longed-for beach.
- How jellyfish only sting people who are at the ocean for a few days.
- How after six days at the beach, my hands became webbed. ... And are those fish scales growing on my legs?

The Summer Son

Who is this man-child who walks beside me on the beach?

I say child, because he is mine, and I say man because he is, in fact, a grown man, age 39. Taller than I, he is slender and wide-shouldered. The thing I notice about him each year is his gentleness. His voice is softer than his brother's and sisters'.

This summer there is a mustache — perhaps to make him look older.

He is a research scientist at a prestigious university and hospital. But, in case you see a Greek god here in mom's eye, he has crow's feet around his eyes, and there is a vertical worry line in the center of his forehead. He is not Robert Redford.

We are walking along the beach where our bare footprints barely make an indent on the wet sand and where the foaming tide like soap bubbles catches our moving feet and shifts between our toes.

The smell and the sounds of the early-morning ocean are a perfect background for our once-a-year visit.

He is my summer son. We get to renew our friendship only during the summer because we live so far apart. And this is the end of summer.

I am having a wonderful time. Like all long-term mothers, I am trying to get reacquainted with this person to whom I gave birth, whom I nurtured and watched over; who, at 12, seemed so open, so carefree. A great sadness for a parent is not being able to se an adult/child frequently. Not to watch him or her grow from adulthood into "middlehood" — that part of their lives when they begin to feel older.

My son lives with his wife and child in another city, and we manage to touch base at Christmas, surrounded by family. At that time, we laugh, joke, sing and eat. But we are as surface ships passing one another. We don't really anchor.

Oh, I can fly to see them, and I do, maybe once a year.

But this is my summer son.

This short vacation is the only time I can get to know him again. There is a fitting feeling of bonding today, here beside the majestic ocean. Does he feel the light touch today of maternal love? Does he feel my yearning? I don't know.

I remember that I am always his mother — such an indestructible label. Mothers never hang up their roles, really. Oh sure, we are the ones who try to cut the apron strings, but we can't cut the tie between the souls.

His life, I know, is full with his exciting work, his family and friends — and that is as it should be.

But who is this summer son, this grown man? Is he all he should be, all we tried to teach him to be?

I want to ask him so many things.

He is a quiet man, not an extrovert like his mother, but he has a twinkle in his eye and has a fine sense of humor. His laughter is deep and contagious.

But who is my summer son? Is he well? Does he love his work or just like it?

We stay on the surface of things with our conversation — like our marching footprints on the tide's edge.

He teases me, and I like that. "Mom, you worry too much. We're all fine."

We talk of current events and then old times and old friends.

I like this, too, but I'm running out of time, and we are running out of beach.

So I start in, carefully. I ask him about his work, too complicated for a lay person or a mother who flunked calculus. I ask him about his house back in their city. Then I ask him what he worries about.

Then I finally unleash my darkest parental questions.

"Darling, how is everything really? Are you OK?"

That sounds cloying — kind of like when he was 10 and on his way to camp. I fence. He parries.

Everything is great, he reassures me.

But is he happy, child of mine, child of the adult world now?

Then I finally ask, "Are you happy?"

I am now infringing on his spirit space. But mothers do that, don't they?

He laughs loudly against the sound of the encroaching tide, then, "Mom, you know what? You asked that last summer, too."

We laugh together.

He is happy. I can tell, can't I?

Then I ethereally glide off like the seagulls that are following us on the beach.

What a question. What is happiness anyway? To each it is something different. And do I really want to hear the wrong answer?

Then I remember with ecstatic joy — there is always next summer!

And I will ask the question again of my summer son.

Summer Grandson

My roommate was so easy to get along with, so amicable. I wondered after the first night where anyone my age could find a roommate so accommodating, so lovable. Where else but in my own family.

My beach roommate this past summer was an 8-year-old — Max.

Where else could I find such big, brown eyes, such new front teeth that enhance a twinkling smile to greet me in the morning?

This year, on our family's annual beach vacation, which includes a rental beach house, I chose Max as my roommate. But I really think he might have chosen me. The others stay up so late and sleep late. Max and I like to greet the day. We seemed to be on a similar time clock.

Where else could I find a sleeping roomie who allows me to read, at least until 10, with the light on? And where else could I find a roomie who places a Luke Skywalker (plastic *Star Wars* figure) on the table between our beds aimed at me for protection during the night?

Where else could I find a roomie whose reading is so diverse from mine that it was funny to see our two current books sitting on our shared small table? My book was "Joy School" by Elizabeth Berg, and his book, published by Oxford University Press, nonetheless, was a scratch-and-sniff book entitled "Tudor Odors" (a mixture of history for 8-year-olds and their spontaneous humor). Then, under his pillow, there might have been "Batman and Robin." Anything to make him read, because he prefers baseball or golf or swimming. And this summer, conquering small waves on his new boogie board.

Needless to say, I love him, and I figure this was the last summer he would room with me. He will soon feel too old to room with his grandmother.

He is so consummately sweet right now and does not yet roll his eyes when I say something like, "Did you finish your yogurt?" or "Where is your other shoe?"

Sometimes he is very literal and corrects me, and that's OK, too, because I know he is learning and testing his intellectual wings. If I tell a story wrong or get a current event askew, he says, "Grraan!" And he sets me straight. Next year, when he gets to be 9, our relationship could change.

Remarks like "Cal Ripken plays third now, Gran" or "Gran, where did you get that funny hat?" are concurrent with his candid attitude and not meant to hurt. I'm sure by 9 he would rather play tag with a friend on the beach. I gave up tag about 10 years ago.

Now, I'm not dumb enough to say he is a Little Lord Fauntleroy. But where else could I find a roommate of such caliber that he allowed me to hug and kiss him good night? And, oh yes, tell him family stories like the time my siblings and I jumped off the garage roof with umbrellas to try to fly. I was 8 then.

Besides having a cool time at the beach with my grown children, I found out something about 8-year-olds. They are mostly honest and unjaded. From the most innocuous of our conversations — about dolphins or his latest ride on his board (triumphant for him, terrorizing for me) — I learned something from him.

I usually worry ahead: Did I turn off the icemaker at home? Will the weather still be okay for my cookout two weeks from now? Or worries like when is my car due for its checkup, and, oh yes, let's not forget about Medicare cuts. Max, however, taught me how to worry just for the moment. His worries are only temporal, short-lived. He might worry where his favorite pillow is, the one he sleeps with in his firm nocturnal grasp.

But he does not worry for his future or the future of the world around him, as we older folks do. It was so beautiful to hear him tell me that he swam near the dolphins and that he would wait for the morning to see more.

He does not worry on a long-term basis about his asthma, because his loving mother has it under control. He asks questions a lot, but they aren't ones of fear and tumult. He sleeps well. Sometimes even before I was finished with my old camp songs, especially all the verses of "Clementine," he was out like a light.

Where else could I find a good friend who wasn't devastated when we could not go boating because of heavy rain, so we went to the boardwalk for wonderful milkshakes? He accepts disappointments and processes them now in a thoughtful way. Ah, the sweet innocence of being 8 and living one day at a time.

How I would love to go to sleep on a special pillow that lulls me into the land of nod and know that I am safe and the world is OK for one more summer night.

And, hopefully, the sun will shine, but if it doesn't, rain is all right, too, he would tell me, or let's just contemplate the next great wave and try to catch it.

The joie de vivre of that age is contagious.

September Song

I'm glad to see the month of September come to its unglamorous end. I found out what it is I don't like about September. It's a time of change and transition. It's a boring steppingstone with boring weather patterns. And it doesn't have soul.

For parents, it's a time of stepping from the hurly-burly of screen doors slamming, telephones ringing, children scrapping and wet bathing suits hanging around to a twilight zone of silence.

They've gone back to school, even though it is still too hot. They come home with glowing tales or tales of woe.

For the working man or woman, it's the end of the vacation season. Gone are the long naps on the sand, late morning sleep-ins, crab feasts, cold beer and the sound of the ocean waves.

You can't even call it Indian summer; it's too soon. It's just been hot, old September.

Someone says to me in the checkout line, "Oh, isn't it great? They've gone back to school, now I can at least play bridge in peace."

No, I say to myself, I miss the laughter and the tears and the peanut butter summer. September spells the death of summer for me. And I always mourn for a short while.

I walk in the September garden. It is bedraggled. The ivy is drying up, the ferns are blanching out from the heat, the roses are confused; some are blooming again. The two pumpkins are puzzled. They are growing, but their color isn't good yet. The worms got to some of my favorite apple trees.

Even the bees swarming over the late-blooming zinnias are mixed up. They are bumping into one another while they grab that last bite of nectar. The scary kudzu vine that was like a green blanket draped over the adjacent meadow is folding up its voracious tentacles for the winter. Only the flies seem to be having fun.

Everyone is rushing into fall clothes, and fall hasn't "fallen."

September smiles slyly down upon us, baking the Earth and laughing at us while we run around and prepare for winter.

Even the poets couldn't find much to write about September. Oliver Wendell Holmes says in his "September Gale," "I am not a chicken; I have seen many a chill September. ...."

But I don't think he was in Baltimore when he wrote it.

From the lovely but mournful "September Song," "... but the days grow short, when you reach September." And I rejoice that the September days are shorter.

Even the sun and Earth are in combat while the metamorphosis of the top-soil begins.

September, like February, is just a month to pass through. A steppingstone to the world of colored leaves and cooler breezes. The promise of a glorious autumn.

Chapter 15

Winter:
the calendar's black hole

All Wrapped Up in Winter's Gray

About this time of year, I get this "pre-winter depression." It is brought on by several factors: one, the sight of the first bare maple tree; two, I've brought in the garden hose and won't be using it again until spring, and three — the worst — I may have to get my winter coat out of its storage bag.

Some like it hot, some like it cold, and I like it hot. It's as simple as that.

In fact, the past few weeks, on cold mornings, I've been wearing my raincoat to work in rebellion against that winter coat.

However, I know where it is, and I have peeked at it once or twice where it hangs so smug, wrapped in that cellophane bag, a fearsome sentinel of winter, harbinger of bad weather and icy roads.

I mean, if I wear it, that means winter has really come and will be here for at least six months, right? The time of the storm windows, antifreeze and snow tires!

And like a cocoon, I will be wrapped in poly and wool waiting and watching until I see the first robin. Then I will unfold like a butterfly and spread my wings once again in delight.

When I open the closet and see that coat, I stick my tongue out at it and those big, fat buttons. I have yelled "g'way," and slammed the door shut. But the coat remains motionless and stubborn, slightly threatening. Its big buttons stare at me like cruel eyes right through the closet door.

The other night, while the wind was howling outside, I confessed to my husband my inner feelings about delaying the wearing of that coat.

He tried to be understanding.

"Look, it is so simple. It's psychological. Buy a new coat. You deserve it. This will help with your problem. Your coat is pretty old. I think you are actually sick of that brown coat and its dullness."

"No, that's giving in to winter and its accouterments. ... Brown coat?" I yell. "It's gray, don't you even remember it?"

"It was brown last year," he says, laughing.

But I'm not laughing. I run to the closet to look. I get it out of its bag. It smells wintery, mothbally and wooly. "It's gray, dummy," I shout.

"Yeah, I guess it is. But see there, I made you get it out. I made you face the fact and the issue. And it's winter. Try it on."

He trapped me. My own husband. I tried it on. ...

And thus was the beginning of winter for me and my gray coat with the big buttons. And with it comes all the slush, mush and gush that cold weather spawns and spews.

Snow Stories at the Checkout

I ran to the grocery store at the beginning of the snowstorm and went zooming through the checkout, buying 16 boxes of Little Friskies, one bottle of vinegar and one encyclopedia, titled "MUR."

"Let's see, you are going to climb into bed, snuggle up with a well-fed cat, drink a bottle of red wine vinegar and read the encyclopedia."

That was the voice of one friendly checkout person with a sense of humor.

"You are almost right," I said. "The cats are out of food, and I thought before we got snowed in I'd better get something for them.

"And I have all your encyclopedias up to MUR. By spring, I will have the whole set," I tell him, smiling.

"And the vinegar?" he asks.

"Well, that's for my hair."

Then he told me how interesting it was to work the fast lane before it snows.

"Most people come in and buy all the staples, in case they get snowbound. But I had one man for years who everytime it stormed came running in to buy a case of Ivory soap."

"You're kidding. He stays in the bathtub?"

"No, he's a whittler. He carves things with the cakes."

"Then I have a woman who is a health food person, and she rushes in and buys up all my fresh vegetables, herbal teas, brown bread, brown rice, yogurt and sunflower seeds. Then later on her husband rushes in and buys pounds of white sugar and white flour, cupcakes and bacon."

I said, "Wow, you can tell a lot about people, can't you, by being a checkout person?"

"Yeah, and snow changes people's personalities. And I'll tell you a secret: Your husband just stopped in and bought some dog food."

"But we don't have a dog," I told him.

"You'd better hurry and get home."

Fighting the Blahs, or Place the Face

The blahs. Do you have them now? They arrive in January or February, and they mainly attack women. They are part of the post-holiday blues and bills.

But there are some things you can do to get rid of them:

1. You can run away with the milkman.
2. You can learn to make your own noodles.
3. You can go on a trip with a credit card, suntan oil and a bikini.
4. You can buy something you can't afford.
5. You can take up basket weaving.
6. You can enroll at a local college and take a course on "How To Make Your Life Broader."
7. Or you can enroll at a reducing salon and find out how to make your body less broad.
8. You can dye your hair or get a facial or any of the 1,001 things open to women today.

OK, I chose the least expensive. The facial. For a new me. I decided to just do it on one side of my face to see public opinion and to see if it was worth going all the way.

So I assaulted the right side with mud packs, cucumber astringent, oil of turtle and every ounce of cosmetics I'd ever bought or been given.

I waxed, polished and buffed. I erased all dark circles, blemishes, warts and almost the entire right side of my face.

We went through our simple two-course meal — that I'd spent five hours preparing — in 20 minutes. No one noticed anything, except that the tea was too strong.

I asked, "Does anyone notice anything different about me?

Here was the reaction:

"You combed your hair for dinner?" And "Mom, you've got on a good dress and no apron."

Finally, I asked, "Which side of my face do you like the best?"

"The left side" (in unison). "The right side looks as if you fell down in the snow while skiing — you look a little, well, blah. And your right eye is slipping."

That did it. While washing the dishes, I steamed off my trial face.

And I made myself a promise. The next day I'd dye my hair fire-engine red. If THEY don't notice, my milkman will. Just wait.

New Year Is Good Time
to Get Rid of Marriage of Bugs

Welcome to the January blahs. But hold on, you can take advantage of them: You can take inventory of your marriage.

My husband and I review our problems, be they small — as in "I wish he'd clip his toenails in the bathroom" — or big — as in "shall we sell the house and move to a condo?"

We find the rap session more therapeutic than hand-to-hand combat, especially coming before tax time.

This methodology is based on the theory adapted by Dr. Sigman Fraud of the Institute of Applied Bioraptics — "argue now, pay later."

So, we don't make New Year's resolutions this time of year; we just write down the things that bug us about one another. (First, of course, we always start the year like every other sofa spud across the nation — trying to diet. We discuss tuna-based dinners and "lite" foods.)

Me: Whoever goes to the store does not buy chips, cheese, cookies or candy.

Agreed.

My husband: Could you refrain from riding the stationary bike while I'm looking at the 6 o'clock news?

Agreed.

Me: If I promise not to use your razor again, could you put the toilet seat down, please?

Agreed.

My husband: Please don't use my comb; I don't like hair spray in my hair.

Agreed.

Me: After you finish the Sunday paper, could you pick it up off the floor?
Agreed.

My husband: Could you stop telling the kids, "Your father's not in good humor, so don't ask him now?"
Agreed.

Me: Could you cook a whole meal, not just the meat, and clean up afterward?
Agreed.

My husband: Promise me you won't make me eat pasta, in any form, more than once a week?
Agreed.

Me: When you write a check, will you try to put the exact amount on the stub in the right column?
Agreed.

My husband: Will you stop doing your yoga in front of the television while I am looking at football, at least for this week?
Agreed.

Me: If we win the lottery, will you promise to take me to the Greek Isles instead of your sister's house in Amarillo?
Agreed.

My husband: Could you pick up your gum wrappers off the floor of the car — at least twice a year?
Agreed.

Me: After you do the laundry, could you put it where it belongs?
Agreed.

By now, I know you're asking: "If it's so easy to agree, why do we ever argue about anything?"

Because we're human, that's why.

Agreed.

Chapter 16

But wait,
I'm not Finished

Excuses, Excuses

The Day Off. It's a glorious-sounding phrase to most of us. To the gainfully employed, it is like the word "bonus" or "winning ticket."

But in late winter, before spring breaks through, the day doesn't bring that certain joy, unless you are a cross-country skier.

Some companies call these personal leave days, slide days, anniversary days. But whatever the term, it means that while you don't have to come to work that day, you get paid.

Great.

I didn't want it to turn out to be a blah day, but blah days are what you make them. Right?

The day fell in the middle of the week, so I couldn't go away for a long weekend. My husband didn't have the same day off, so we couldn't fly to Greece. As a matter of fact, I couldn't even drive to East Trenton, because of the weather forecast.

I couldn't share the day with any of the kids. They were all in school or working. And wouldn't it be weird to spend the day with your mother-in-law unless she were sick?

So I contemplated the things I should do. Spend the day with my mother-in-law, clean out the toaster tray, rearrange the mothballs in my sweater drawer, go through my husband's socks and finally match them up, throw out the old prescription bottles. Yucky.

Then I contemplated the things I wanted to do, in the manner of the books "Erroneous Zones" or "Looking Out for Number One."

•Go to lunch with Paul Newman (he was out of town).

•Go have a facial (would have to work on my face before I got there).

•Have a party (too much trouble).

•Play bridge (haven't played in 22 years).

•Eat lunch with a good friend (they were all working or having the flu).

•Go sketch a certain tree on a hill (I've been meaning to do this for years, but better to do it in the spring).

•Tour a museum (more fun to do this with someone else who loves art).

•Go to a movie alone (have not done that since "Smiling Through").

•Go buy that expensive dress I'd seen in a downtown window (income tax has not yet been determined).

•Curl up in bed with a good book while eating sugared almonds (too many calories).

OK. I blew it. I guess. I called my husband and told him that since I didn't want to have a blah day off, I'd take him to lunch.

"Roy Rogers is closed for repairs," he said snidely.

I told him I'd treat him to that new Greek restaurant.

"Better still, I'll come home for lunch and bring the spinach pies from the place," he whispered.

He didn't understand. I wanted an assignation away from the house. And I really wanted to see those murals of Greece on the walls and dream.

But the spinach pies, the sugared almonds and the book were great.

Blah can be beautiful.

The Post-Reunion Blues

Thirty-one-year-old Jenny went to her first class reunion the other day. She came home depressed.

She told me all about it. "They just weren't doing what they set out to do. They copped out ... it shows education in the late 1960s was not relevant and a waste of time for some of them."

I asked, "Like who does what now?"

She explained. "Take Rap Golden, who threw himself in front of the Nixon motorcade to protest the war. I was so proud of him. But now he's working in defense making nuclear machinery. He wears three-piece suits and has a crew cut.

"And Barry Mansfield. He was our class president, honor society, captain of the football team — a real square, but he had beautiful eyes. Well, he's chanting and selling flowers at airports, dressed in purple robes.

"Then there were the Cleaver twins — they always were ahead of the times. They stole all the fur coats from the dorms and took them to Goodwill to protest the extinction of the Alaskan seals. ... Then, as I remember, they streaked the Whopper Bowl game and were later expelled.

"Now, they're both married to bank executives, and Millicent is a high school vice principal. They live in Suburbia Hills and have Tupperware parties.

"I'm disgusted. Where are all the beliefs we fought for?"

She went on, "And there's Emma Lou Duderry, who was practically my best friend. She was our campus ecumenical director. Now she is starring in porno films and has had six husbands. ..."

"Look, Jenny," I interjected, "I think they've come full circle. Change is good for people. I just read in *Time* magazine that the kids of the 1960s are making an excellent mark on the present-day business world — that is, those who weren't hurt or imprisoned during the turbulence. I think it's great.

"What was your major, Jenny? I've forgotten."

"I was one of the first women to graduate from the school of engineering," she said as she folded her 26th diaper and rescued a box of Girl Scout cookies from her 10-year-old. "But I did rewire the dishwasher. I love doing what I'm doing," she said, a bit defensively.

"But, dear," I said, a bit guardedly, "Maybe they do, too."

The Ambience in Restaurants
Is Either Feast or Famine

Time was when you went to a restaurant, picked up the menu, read it and ordered. But like everything else in life, that facet of earthly enjoyment has become more complicated, sort of "high tech-y" or "high tacky."

It was our anniversary, and we had picked out a special, elegant restaurant that was highly recommended.

We were shown to a table by a handsome young man with a frozen smile, who gave us menus so heavy I could hardly hold mine.

We could tell the restaurant had gone chic. (You know, the waiters and waitresses look like models and have drama department accents, and the maitre d' has a two-way radio in the pocket of his three-piece suit.)

Two minutes into reading the menu, and I felt a presence at my elbow. A sprite or a leprechaun? The waiter was costumed and had wonderfully white teeth in his smile and a sing-songy lilt to his voice.

"Good evening, I'm Donnie. (They never give their last names, which I would be much more interested in, as I might know their parents.) I'll be your waiter for this evening."

I have to say I would never call a waiter by his first name, as in, "Oh, Don, how about some more radishes?" And what do they do when their names are strange, like Allouette or Mary Josephine?

Anyway, he went on.

"The specials tonight are. ..." and he began a spiel as long and flowery as a recitation in a fifth-grade assembly.

"The stuffed flounder a la de Gaulle is made with orange sauce pablona, and is filled with chopped shrimp in a buttered embellishment of water chestnuts, minced tongue and ..."

Because I can read and so can my husband, we wondered why the restaurant didn't just give us a piece of paper and let us look at the specials. I started to nod off during his briefing, but he finally finished.

"And the piece de resistance (pronounced wrong) is a steak de nuit with Rhine wine mushrooms and chili peppers."

My husband whispered to him, "What do you have in a four-wheel drive with power steering?"

But that didn't deter Donnie. "And the dessert specials are ..."

Finally I asked sweetly, "Would it be possible to have some water with our dinner?"

That made him forget his spiel, and suddenly I felt sorry for him. It isn't easy to memorize the specials in an ever-changing society with ever-changing meals, especially when you are working to put yourself through medical school or trying to support a wife and three children whose idea of food is a fat french fry.

With the mention of water, I could have sworn the waiter said, "Oh yes, that's very popular tonight."

"But it's not a special," I said, trying to make him laugh. He didn't laugh, but he kept on smiling.

Right there and then, I was determined to give him a 25 percent tip. All that memorizing had to be rewarded.

Now ask me, was the dinner good? Yes, the dinner was good. We didn't order the specials, for which I felt guilty. But Donnie seemed omnipresent, like a nurse in intensive care.

And three times during the first part of the dinner, he asked if he could remove the appetizer plate, the salad plate, the dinner plate and our ashtray. He also forgot about the water.

If you want to be alone with your date or husband at this type of restaurant, forget it, there's just not enough time.

All this made me wonder why restaurants don't start using a table computer, or go back to posting the specials on a chalkboard. Of course, they could go the other way and have the waitress or waiter sit down with you and discuss the entire menu while having a drink.

You know, "Hello, my name is Roselyn Brigokowski and I am 24. I graduated with honors with a degree in anthropology, but have not found a job. So I am now going to graduate school in computer sciences. But until I get a job out there, I will be waitressing. I meet interesting people this way. Are you interesting? My hobbies are ..."

But then why are we complaining? There are restaurants whose service is so bad you wish you could get up and run.

But isn't there something in between? Something between fast food and Chasens? Something between chic and old shoes?

Stamping Out the 'How To'

Did you ever get to thinking that we don't know how to do anything?

Well, apparently we don't — if you believe the number of "how to" books in print.

If your sex life is no good or your spaghetti sauce isn't up to par, you can just go buy a "how to" book. There's something for everyone.

There are about 3,000 this year in print.

There are so many, you may be psychologically intimidated by the "how to" syndrome. I mean, you're scared to potty train your 7-year-old, because a "how to" book told you to "go slowly."

The fast-growing market of how tos could be a vast symptom of our growing insecurity.

While looking them up in the books-in-print index, I found that the largest category was the how to make money type. Then I'd say the how to live with type, anything with how to live with your husband, lover, peace of mind, to your neurotic dog.

Here's just a sample: "How to Turn Plastic into Gold," "How to Be a Genius," "How to Avoid Alimony," "How to Use Peat Moss."

I like the ones dealing in personality traits: "How to Be Offensive to Practically Everybody" — and I know lots of people who don't need to read that one. "How to Marry a Married Man" — weird, but wouldn't it be better if he got a divorce first?

Then here's the kind I really wonder about. "How to Attract the Wombat" — who cares, and what is it anyway?

"How to Wave Your Arms in Front of a Singing Crowd" — any politician or hyper 3-year-old can do that.

"How to Tie Flies" — I trust they mean fishing flies, since most clothing utilizes the zipper-type fly.

"How to Grip-Dip Oscillators" — how does that grab you? This should be in the mystery book category.

OK, want to know how to stamp out "how to" books and get back to doing things your own way? Don't read them. Do it yourself. That is, whatever it is you don't know how to do.

Dream of House Redecoration Turns into a Nightmare

I had a dream. I dreamed that *McCall's* magazine came and redecorated my whole house for free.

You see, right before I went to bed, I read in the September issue that the magazine had selected a winner in its "Reader of the Year Contest" to subsequently get her home remodeled and herself, too.

They received more than 10,000 letters from applicants. To make the final selection, the magazine judged which readers and homes the magazine would best lend themselves to demonstration of the magazine's departments and services — decorating, beauty, fashion, food and management and so forth.

Well, this nice-looking couple was selected and this month there are pictures in the magazine of all the great things that were done to them and their house.

But my dream turned into sort of a nightmare.

First of all, I must tell you I'm eligible for such a prize. Some of our furniture dates back 38 years, not old enough to be antique, but not young enough to look good. Stuff from early marriage to Golden Pond. Springs pop up in sofas in the wrong place. It takes pliers to turn on the TV. Faucets have strings attached to them so they won't drip. Appliances have to be kicked to start.

So in my dream, I was selected and began running around, trying to make our place look better before the magazine crew descended.

I vacuumed under beds I've never looked under. I threw away all my polyester stretch pants that were so tight I could trace my dinner. I pitched the ashtray that says "Welcome to Carlsbad Caverns" and the rug that says "Maryland is for Crabs."

I cleaned the oven and the fridge with a Q-tip. I threw all the clothes I could find in the washing machine, along with the kids' hub cap collection, and unplugged it. (For years, I've had to throw myself on it when it's "spinning/dry" to keep it from walking out of the utility room.)

I threw away two disreputable-looking mattresses and made the beds up over the box springs. I painted the leaves of the philodendron green and waxed my driveway.

I wanted to look clean and deserving, but poor enough to need help. I wanted my house to be a challenge, you know.

I mean, a home management editor was going to come and tell me how to make crepes with my right hand while curling my hair with my left. And how to get the kids to do their chores without threatening their lives, their stereos and their allowances.

Finally, in my dream the big day came, and this crew of people trooped into our average American, mortgaged, muddled home.

I was dressed in my best go-to-the-grocery-store-and-will-you-cash-my-check-outfit, with just the right amount of makeup to make them feel there was some hope but that it would take time and lots of money.

What happened? You would think I might have collapsed from "housework" exhaustion and the team of experts would have trundled me out on a stretcher.

But no. In my dream, my husband came home early and announced he'd been transferred out of town and told *McCalls* to call the whole thing off.

I woke up in a cold sweat and nudged my husband awake to tell him about the dream.

He told me to please read the *National Geographic* before I go to sleep at night.

If You Don't Have a Trap,
Try a Little Legal Tender

I'm not one of those squeamish women. I mean, if I see a mouse I don't run and jump on a chair like some women. I don't faint if I see a snake in the garage.

In fact, if it's alive I'll pick it up, but if it's dead I'm reluctant. I've picked up live daddy long legs, moving caterpillars on little girls' dresses, inch worms off collars and I captured a neighbor's runaway cow in our backyard. You can note, therefore, I am brave, so why can't I catch a mouse, like other people do?

When it gets cold, we usually have two or three mice that settle in with us for the long, cozy winter. They are not city mice or foreign mice, just field mice, I tell myself. But other people manage to catch them in traps or by poison — this just doesn't work at our house. Our mice like that powdered poison. They manage to get the cheese out of the trap without springing the trap, in fact, they dance around the trap in triumph with cheese in their little teeth.

Would you believe we have two cats? We've tried every combination of cats, hoping they'd get the mice. We've tried two males, so that they might portray feline chauvinism and conquer. We've tried two females, who we figured would fight between themselves and get hungry. We tried one female and one male, hoping their sex life would "rev" them up enough to chase mice or that after procreation their offspring would eat mice.

Right now, we have two fixed females, named Cat and Kitty. Although they have been known to eat anything, including dog food, table food, pizza, lettuce with french dressing — they won't eat mice.

Some smarty said, "Starve those cats, they'll get the mouse." I did. And on the third day, the cats were eating the rug pad.

This one mouse has become so brazen that the other night he was sitting up staring at me from a cabinet. I said to him, "Wait a minute," and he did. I went and got Cat. Cat stared at the mouse, winked and started bathing. If I could "bell" the mouse, I think the cat would get him. Anyway, up until now you haven't believed a word I've said, and from now on you won't either.

I've found a way to catch a mouse in the house. I put out a $5 reward. I told the cats, the kids, the mouse and even the two dogs, I even mentioned it to the milkman.

Last week, I came home to a large carton in the living room with 6 or 7 kids looking into the box.

Now, it's too late for Easter, I thought, and I told them last year no more baby ducks.

I looked in. There he was. He smiled up at me, he was really cute.

"Can we keep him, Mom?"

"Are you kidding? Take him outside, tell him his rights and set him free, he'll be back."

The Friendly Smile Closes with the Elevator's Doors

You can feel awfully lonely in a crowded elevator. In these days of nude encounter groups and touching theories, why are people so distant in elevators? Some people are downright unfriendly in elevators.

The other day I stepped into a packed elevator. No one smiled. People looked as if they were going to a funeral. We picked up a man on the third floor — there wasn't any room for him, but I tried to move back. He had just walked in and said "10." And then he stood facing me — it was so crowded he couldn't turn around. We were nose to nose, if you know what I mean. I will say this, he did fold his hands, so I folded mine, but he didn't smile.

There ought to be a code for elevator behavior. Now I don't think you ought to jump right in and all hold hands, but along with no littering there ought to be lots of laughter and at least a bunch of smiles.

Have you ever noticed how some people get in the elevator and don't move back, and some move toward the sides, turn and just stare.

So when I got home, I called my psychiatrist friend and asked him, "What is wrong with a man who doesn't turn around and face the door in an elevator?"

"Well, he could be a sex maniac."

"No, he folded his hands."

"As in prayer?"

"No, like he had a stomach ache. ..."

"Then he probably did."

Then he went on to tell me that many people have elevator sickness or claustrophobia. Many people hate elevators. They don't trust them, he explained.

He has also found that people who look upward when they ride in an elevator are optimists and people who look down at the floor are pessimists.

I told him about my friend Ginny, who was stuck in an elevator the other day between the fifth and sixth floors with one man who never said, "Boo." Ginny became panic-stricken and pushed all the buttons at one time and screamed and even climbed the walls. Twenty minutes later, the elevator moved. Ginny reports the man just stood in the corner.

I asked my doctor friend what is wrong with a man like that. He said, "Nothing," something was wrong with Ginny.

In Dallas, Houston, Atlanta (in elevators that I've known), people say "good morning" or "hello."

Here in the East, if you say "How are you today?" they look at you as if you'd said, "Come up and see me sometime."

How I'd hate to get caught in an elevator during a power failure on the East Coast. And yet I heard that during the big failure in New York City, a bunch of people spent all night in the elevators.

A rescue team climbed down the shaft to help with any emergencies and called, "Is anyone pregnant down there?" and some jester yelled back, "Not yet."

Well, I don't believe it. I will bet the people spent the night standing up straight and looking straight forward singing, "We Shall Overcome." Because I've never even been pinched in an elevator.

Dawn Can Be Special on Easter Morning

I begged the doctors to let me go home in an ambulance just for the day. The answer was no, and I'm sure they were right.

After about two weeks in the hospital, I couldn't sit up and still was in great pain.

I'd had a spinal fusion, a back operation, and had been flat on my back. They had told me if my special brace came I would be able to go home by Easter.

I had made the mistake of looking at my watch. It was about 5, Easter morning. The hospital was pretty quiet. Many patients had gone home for the weekend, and most of the staff were given the day off.

When I first awoke, I felt that terrible blanket of depression that comes from being alone and sick, especially on a holiday. The whole operation came back to me — the pain, the transfusions, the IV feedings, the anxiety over whether it would be a success. The hospital room seemed like an ominous cave of darkness. I closed my eyes and waited for the dawn.

Throughout our marriage, we had shared in our illnesses. Always when I had reached across the pillow, he was there. And that special morning I reached for his hand across the whiteness of the hospital bed, and there was nothing. I became even more childish in my introspection. Thoughts like "Maybe I'll never get out of this hospital," and doubts like "Will I ever really lead a normal life again after this operation?" crossed my mind in surging waves of self-pity.

Then, too, I have always loved Easter. It was a special time for me. It meant the end of winter, new beginnings — the most meaningful time to get my spirituality back on track.

I tried in vain to go back to sleep. But it was Easter morning, and my thoughts turned back to home — the dawn would be coming up over my house, too. What was going on there? The memories of other Easters came back to me.

Probably no one was even awake that early. But the Easter bunny used to be when the kids were young. Images of the search to find the Easter eggs, the wonder of the first daffodil, the fragrance of Easter lilies in the church rituals engulfed me.

The sounds of my own house — I missed them all. A hospital is a sterile place. I knew I was being peevish, but when you are weak, the worst comes out in you.

And then I thought of all the other sick and, yes, dying people who were in the hospital. And I said a prayer for them that Easter morning. But their plight only added to my depression.

I wasn't meant to sit up or stand up yet, although I had stood up twice, when no one was looking, to test my strength..

Suddenly, I had to stand. Tears of self-pity were coming down my cheeks, and it was time to move.

I looked out the large smeary winter-weary window, and I saw the first signs of a glorious dawn — something much larger than my personal misery. The sky had turned a bright pink, then orange and the tall, mirrored buildings were echoing the luminous hues of the rising sun. My door opened, and an aide I'd never seen before moved quietly toward me. She said, "Happy Easter, child, He has risen, He has risen ... and joy to you."

She put her arms around me. She was tall — she was from Jamaica, she told me later — so her voice had that beautiful lilting quality.

She was what I needed. She saw my tears, and her face lit up with encouragement — "That is good, you stand, that is good. Then I help you back in bed."

For one brief minute, we stood next to one another and watched the dawn as it exploded into the day.

She missed her family, too — they were in Jamaica. She was auxiliary help at the hospital on holidays. She was not dispensing kindness and love on this Easter day.

It was her strength, her touch, that transfixed me with human gladness. I forgot myself. And, suddenly, I knew I would make it. And I did get out of the hospital four days later.

She gave me a special Easter.

And I wonder if she knew that the word Easter comes from "Eastre" meaning "dawn goddess."

Sibling Rivalry Among Adults

It was after the winter holidays that I kept hearing it, that having all the grown children home at one time brings out the worst in families.

Anna was wringing her hands over an age-old subject — sibling rivalry. "It was awful this Christmas. I'm not sure I can go through that again, there was so much tension."

She and I were trying to fathom the depth of sibling rivalry and why it seems to be more rampant after they grow up and have their own families.

Perhaps it's because family members are more spread out geographically, so when they infrequently get together, the impact is greater and a lot of baggage comes down the pike.

Anna, who has a big family, told me, "There were snide remarks behind one another's backs, things like, 'I can't stand her political views or her hairdo.'

"Or I'd hear, 'Well, sure they have a new car, his salary is now six figures. Or 'If she stayed home with her kids more, they'd be better behaved.'

"Believe me," Anna added, "the kids never seemed as rivalrous when they were growing up as they do now. Something has happened, and I worry about after I'm gone, will they be nicer to one another?"

I agree with her that large families incur petty jealousies and idiosyncrasies, and it does seem to be more prevalent as the children get older and branch out into more economic and social diversity.

In a telephone interview from Amherst, Mass., I talked to a longtime friend, Jenifer McKenna, a psychotherapist in private practice, who herself came from a large and loving family.

Jenifer said that from Thanksgiving to Christmas or Hanukkah, the sibling rivalry and stress in her clients' families was more pronounced.

Her insights: "The rivalry is just a piece of the action; the whole thing stems from childhood. The perceived rivalry just changes form. Where there has been anger and hostility between siblings based on past memories and the years of struggle within the family framework, there is renewed competition.

"Even in adulthood, the birth order is still significant. The baby, be she 16 or 30, is still the baby. Even if you don't have a lot in common with your older sister or you don't see eye-to-eye with her, when you come into the room and she is there, you will notice there is an inherent interlocking feeling.

"Just knowing my older sister is in the world makes me feel safer. There's a powerful heartstring pull. And when the chips are down, siblings usually will defend each other. And remember, the good times usually outweigh the tough times."

The counselor said that there is even more change when in-laws or grandchildren come into the picture. "Whereas we take liberties with siblings, we don't with in-laws. The materialism rivalry is just a symbol of the past — who got the most affection or gifts or who is the prettiest. Then when the grandchildren come along, it's which one is getting the most attention from the grandparents. All this is not unusual."

She suggested that big families get together at other times because Christmas and Hanukkah are stressful times by themselves.

Coincidentally, a recent *McCall's* has an article: "Mending broken family ties: How to get close again."

Duke University's Deborah Gold stated: "Strained relationships with brothers and sisters are among the most common but difficult-to-admit problems adults experience. But, as they mature, most express a real need to have a brother or sister as a friend."

How to mend the rivalries?

The article suggested that you might have to view your parents as one-time children and understand how their rearing influenced the ways they treated you and your siblings. Letter-writing was recommended and is most effective when it's a series of "I" messages, or if your sister's husband is the main reason you are upset, try to build a just-you-and-me-relationship, meeting for lunch or exchanging funny cards.

The magazine summed up that as you help the child within you grow up, you may feel more secure about reaching out to an estranged brother or sister.

And most experts agree you should forgive someone who is unrepentant, because the very act of forgiving heals you. But remember that forgiving does not necessarily mean forgetting.

I have a feeling that in our mobile and rapidly changing society, older siblings can become a comforting resource to one another and that within the circumferences of family dynamics, we should work for better acceptance, understanding and love.

My Young Inquisitive Friend

I was on a jet zooming home from Dallas when I found myself being inter-
viewed. Not by a reporter, but by a 5-year-old girl with a beguiling smile.

A 5-year-old, whose name was Amy, became my seatmate while her little
brother, Paul, was getting airsick across the aisle. Her mother and father
were trying to cope with the baby. I told them not to worry, I'd keep Amy's
mind off the baby, the mess and the rough flight. I had an empty seat next to
mine. But it seems Amy did the talking. Well, mostly.

Her first question was, had I ever been airsick? I said no. I also told her
I'd been on hundreds of planes and I'd lived to be 72, see!

The rest of the interview was in a Q-and-A mode. I will try to reconstruct.

Amy: This is my first airplane ride. I think you are older than my granny.

Me : Well, I'm old, but I don't feel old. Especially in the morning when I
get up, I forget how old I am.

Amy : Yeah, the only reason I could tell that you were older was that you
have a lot of brown spots on your hands and arms. She doesn't have any yet.

Me : Yes, I do. They come from being in the sun before we had sunscreen,
and I have them on my face, too.

Amy : I don't see so many on your face. (She smiled before continuing.)
Just some wrinkles, but they are small, don't worry.

She paused then asked, "Did you eat a lot of candy all your life, because
they don't let me eat a lot of sugar."

Me : Well, no. Well, some. But I don't eat a lot now. I love chocolate, and
I eat it maybe once a week.

Amy : Were you a swimmer?

Me : Yes, I was when I was young. I loved tennis the best.

Amy : I want to learn tennis, but I am taking ballet now. Did tennis make you feel good?

Me : Yes, I think anything you love that you do makes you feel good. (Whoa, I thought to myself, am I on the right course with this? Would this get her parents' approval?)

Amy : Did you get a lot of sleep when you were young? Did you have to go to bed early? (Be careful here, I cautioned myself.)

Me : Yeah, I love to sleep. Sometimes, I went to bed early on school nights.

Amy : Maybe that's what makes you have the energy to fly in a jet. I have to go to bed at 7:30 in the winter.

She was quiet for a while, then suddenly she asked me, "Do you ever feel you're gonna die, because you are old, uh, older?"

Me : No, I don't think a lot about death. I worry when older people die, especially those I love. But death is part of life. Sometime I will die. But I try to eat right and exercise and stay well.

Amy : Well, I don't think you are going to die either. My grandmother has an illness, and she says she wants to die.

Me : Well, maybe she is in pain, but she really just wants to feel well, don't you think?

Amy : I don't like to see people die, especially on television, so I don't look at it much.

Me : (on a roll now) I think you should do everything in moderation, like don't eat too much candy and get a lot of exercise, and don't look at television too much.

Amy : You are right. Mom only lets me look at it for a half-hour a day.

Me : Sounds like you have wonderful parents.

Amy : I guess. (Then just a smile.) I hope I won't be sick like Paul, because we are going to see New York.

Me : No. You won't be sick. Think about something nice and close your eyes.

But the interview was not really over. She closed her eyes, but would look at my hands when her eyes opened.

Amy : (suddenly) Your fingernails are sort of yellow, now what does that mean?

Me: That means I didn't put on any nail polish before I got on the plane. Want me to tell you the story of Cinderella or Jack and the Beanstalk?

She voted for 101 Dalmatians of which my knowledge was skimpy. And then it was time to land. Paul was asleep as we scooted bumpily down the runway.

As I gathered up my things, I was reminded how knowing yet innocent, how intuitive, yet how vulnerable children are at that age. I also realized I wasn't in such bad shape, that I "had the energy to fly in a jet" and that I did not think I wanted to die yet. Amy reminded me to think positively. I learned a lot from Amy.

Did I teach her anything? Probably not.

We said goodbye. Her mother thanked me and told me Amy's grand-mother was 54. Then, at the baggage claim, Amy whispered to me with a smile, "Don't forget to wear your sunscreen."

Flying the Friendly Skies Between Parents

I want to tell you about a boy I'll call Bobby. In some ways he is a special boy, a child of the 1980s. And I'm not going to make you sad.

On the contrary, I will make you glad. Glad that you can find kids like Bobby out there.

Bobby traveled with me on a plane across the country. He was my seatmate.

He was flying to Baltimore from Dallas.

Bobby was 8-years-old, I found out much later. He was small for his age, and thin, neatly dressed with a huge digital watch that he looked at a lot.

He was curled up in the window seat when I took my place in the aisle seat. There was an empty seat between us.

His eyes were deep set, a beautiful dark brown, flecked with amber lights. But his eyes had a kind of wariness, like a deer's. He would look me over with timidity and a certain soulfulness. He had the lovely skin of a pre-adolescent and curly brown hair that he will probably hate later.

Of course, he had been told not to talk to strangers, you could tell that.

After my original "Hi," the one reserved for seatmates until they warm up or cool off, I kept my distance for a while.

There was a certain quiet aura about Bobby. This handsome, little guy seemed relaxed yet coiled for action.

If you think I fell in love with him, well, I did.

As I've said, I left him alone at first. He seemed so self-sufficient. When the flight attendants started serving lunch, he uncurled.

I ventured: "How far are you going?" Not too many questions at first.

"I'm going to Baltimore — to my dad's for the summer."

Oh, I got the picture. He was going to Dad's because his parents are divorced. That explains the traveling alone. His Mom lives in another state. Sure, that's it.

In fact, I had just read that this summer the airlines expect about half a million children, most of them between parents.

I tried to pull my tray out of the armrest.

Bobby leaned over and helped me. He even unfolded the tray across my lap and the tray for the empty seat between us.

"This way we can have more room for our food," he said, smiling.

"Wow, you seem to have traveled quite a bit," I said. He'd already adjusted his air vent and managed to get a pillow from the overhead storage. "Oh, I have. I've been, let's see, at least four times across the country. I go to my Dad's on holidays, Christmas, Easter, but not on Halloween. I love to fly."

My mother-heart turned over. The poor, little kid. He seemed so small, so vulnerable, to be traveling alone so many times. What happened to the marriage? Will he miss his mom this summer?" How does his Dad take care of him during the day? Is his mom home crying now? Did she cry all the way home from the airport?

No more questions for now. I promised myself.

While we ate, I commented on how glad I was that the dessert was chocolate.

That did it, we became friends. He opened up.

"Usually, it is chocolate on Delta. I love chocolate, too. ... Guess where my Dad is taking me this summer? HersheyPark, Pennsylvania. Because I am a choc-o-holic. I can make a chocolate pie, and I can make pasta. ... Dad's also taking me to the beach, and maybe to New York City. He is taking off three weeks this summer.

From then on, Bobby explained his whole life to me.

That his daddy belongs to a swimming pool and Bobby will stay at the pool under supervision on nice days; that his daddy brought a VCR so they can see a lot of Disney movies; that his grandmother lived nearby; that his daddy works short hours in the summer. He's a salesman and gets home early in the afternoon; that Bobby makes his own bed and his father's bed.

But I still anguished.

Is his mother home from the airport now? Is the breathing a sigh of relief that she will be free for the summer?" Or is she crying as she finds a small sock under his empty bed and has to put it away for a long, long time?

I asked Bobby if he likes living in two places.

Long pause.

"It's great. I have two houses, two closets and two sets of toys. I have two sets of friends, and I can see more grandparents this way."

I could tell he loved both parents. He did not seem to be torn between them.

Much later, I was almost glad when he bit his fingernails when the plane came in for a landing — a very normal kid, that boy.

To say Bobby was mature seems sort of condescending — he was just very well-adjusted.

Don't worry, parents of the Bobbys out there, your kids are doing great.

Hospital Visitors are Often More Trouble than Help

Hospital visitors basically fall into two groups.

Group A consists of people who like going to see people in hospitals because there is a mystique for them about illness and operations. These people love hospitals — probably from watching all those episodes of "Ben Casey" and "Dr. Kildare" on television.

And then they feel they are helping the imprisoned hospital friend — the one given directions not to drink any water for eight hours, the one with the roommate who has too many visitors and emits strange sounds night and day.

Group A visitors also feel a certain smugness, a "thank God it's not me" attitude that permeates their visit. They show it when they pat you on your fresh incision or try to adjust your pillows and jostle your head in the process.

Then there's Group B. It is only out of sheer willpower that Group B visitors manage to get to the hospital in the first place, but they hate every minute of the visit.

They despise the smells, the sounds and the sights, and, in fact, they usually live in daily fear of being roped into going to the hospital on a stretcher any minute of any day.

Believe me, both A and B types are not good visitors, but then, even St. Christopher, Bishop Tutu or Moses would not meet the "perfect visitor" standards in most cases.

Having just spent hours with a family member who had his gall bladder removed, I feel authorized to tell you that A and B visitors mean well, but can be a hindrance to both the patient and the hospital staff.

Group A will stay too long, gab too much, talk to the nurses, the cleaning crews and usually like a word with the doctor and a recap of the operation — down to the enema part.

Mostly, they ask the patient too many questions when the patient needs every ounce of strength he or she can muster just to reach for the phone.

Group B visitors, who hate hospitals, stay too short a time. They watch the clock, lie to the patient and say, "You'll up in no time." Their optimism is incredibly debilitating to the patient, who has to figure out how to urinate without a catheter when the visitor's back is turned.

Group B people hope they never have to visit the hospital, an institution of horrors and high-tech equipment, or listen to tired-looking doctors say things like, "We'll do the best we can" or "We'll have to take more tests."

Group B visitors do not understand that surgery is followed by burping, moaning and leaking and that the patient is not held back by social etiquette when doing any of the above.

Fidgety Group B people often bring too many gifts: things like *National Geographic* (featuring stories about animals that eat other animals), *Guide Post* (with messages about how to suffer in dignity) or magazines with articles about "unnecessary surgery," a toothbrush that turns into a flashlight, but doesn't have the batteries included, or a small game with marbles that roll onto the floor if activated.

And all of this when all the patient really needs is a nice card, a smile and a doctor who says, "We don't need to do the surgery, you can go home and play 18 holes of golf."

Group A visitors, who love to visit hospitals, are a bit inclined to hypochondria. They will not only diagnose what you have, but they will also talk about their own ailments and those of their friends and family, everything from an infected hangnail to the gory details of the delivery of their cousin's triplets and the ensuing malpractice suit.

Send flowers or send yourself, but if you go, be sure to call first — and then try to fall somewhere between group A and B.

Hurry Sickness: You May Be Its Latest Victim

Have you heard of the latest illness plaguing busy people? It's "hurry sickness," or "HS," as they are calling it in pop psychology circles.

I am glad this phenomenon is finally out in the open.

Psychologist Dr. Bruce A. Baldwin, author of "It's All in Your Head: Lifestyle Management Strategies for Busy People," defines hurry sickness as "a pervasive sense of urgency that is concerned solely with completion of tasks without regard for the other aspects of experience." I read excerpts from Dr. Baldwin's book in a USAir magazine, while flying 37,000 feet over Cleveland. I never waste time in flight.

To see HS at full effect, just drive on the Washington beltway during rush hour or go to Macy's during a sale or watch people try to get on a plane at the last minute.

Some people, like mothers, air-traffic controllers and editors who put out a daily paper, require HS. I even know retirees who have HS. They run from one hobby to another. And a couple of 2-year-olds I know have it; they run from pulling out the pans in the kitchen to hiding car keys under the sofa.

I think HS is contagious. Dr. Baldwin says it can be inherited.

I've suffered from HS.

I had it when my four children were in four different schools and I had four car pools. I was frenzied most of the time. Life was too full.

I was commuting for 30 minutes on the Beltway to a newspaper job, always hoping to get home before the kids got off the school buses and had time to kill each other over how to split the last of the soda. I was keeping house, working full time and trying to figure out if "that's all there is," as Peggy Lee used to croon.

I often put the salt in the fridge and the butter in the kitchen cabinet. Once, while hurrying to a Little League game, I left a child in a filling station bathroom as I shoved the rest of the kids in the car. When I drove back, I found that, in 10 minutes, he learned how to pump gas.

OK, how do you know if you have it?

Among Dr. Baldwin's signs of HS are:

• Driving patterns: You drive faster than you used to. You rail out at gross incompetence.

• Eating habits: You eat faster to get bigger bites. You eat while driving.

• Communication style: You don't have enough time to give emotional encouragement to others around you.

• Lifestyle: less family involvement, less leisure activities.

In other words, when you're not doing something productive, you experience anxiety and guilt.

So how do you cure HS?

Dr. Baldwin says, "Learn to slow down and not schedule things close together. Accept the problems and delays as part of life. The drive to get ahead is the root of the problem. Achievement-oriented men and women love time-management strategies. Try to enjoy experiences, not rewards."

I say listen and learn from that old saying, "The hurrier I go, the behinder I get."

Chapter 17

Starve a cold

Feed a family

When a Husband Takes Over and Cooks for His Sick Wife

If you are a married woman, you may have experienced a time in your marriage when you were laid up and your husband had to cook. I think every married couple should go through this phase in order to appreciate one another.

I just did. It was a revelation. You come away knowing one of these things:

- That your husband adores you and would turn the kitchen upside down for you.
- That he would turn you upside down and save the kitchen.
- That you need a new husband.
- That militant feminists are right when they say men just are not catching on in the kitchen.

First, let me say my spouse tried to be helpful. He is kind and good. Yet he has really cooked only party food or Sunday barbeques. (You know, "Honey, the steaks are ready, hurry up and bring the rest of the meal out here.")

I was ordered to bed for a few weeks by my doctor because I hurt my back.

My husband started out like a house afire. He brought trays to the bed, a kind of meals on heels. The first night, the dinner tray was one of the pretty ones we'd received for a wedding present but had never used. There was a real napkin, the kind you have to iron, a silver knife and fork, a porcelain plate with stuffed flounder and a fresh salad with his homemade dressing. And oh, yes, cut-up fruit, not canned.

I lay back after the meal and took a pain pill and looked up at the ceiling and said, "Thank you, Lord, for such a fine husband."

The second night, he switched over to paper plates and paper cups, but he came home early and made one of my favorites, stuffed zucchini. And there was a piece of buttered bread on the side. The meal was good.

Then, the next night, something snapped. We started having only meals he likes. He loves chicken wings and can never get enough. So we had chicken wings with peas. And the next night, we had more chicken wings with left-over peas. He loves turnips, and so the next night on the plate — there was no tray under the plate — were turnips and two large, peeled carrots. A rabbit would have been in heaven.

As I recall, the night after that we had undercooked black-eyed peas and rhubarb, one of his favorite dishes.

Then finally, about the eighth night, he heated up a frozen macaroni and cheese. It was great. We split it. I ate right from the container and he got the plate.

Subsequent nights, we ate frozen spinach souffle or frozen scalloped potatoes, using plastic spoons.

Toward the end of my entrapment, we had a grand finale of frozen dinners. He cooked a Mexican dinner, a turkey dinner with a frozen peach pie. But they each took different heating times, so alarms were going off at different intervals, and he was running back and forth. The meal took three hours to eat.

Finally, one night, came the denouement: He forgot dinner altogether. We were looking at TV and it got to be 9 o'clock. I saw a commercial for chewing gum and said, "Honey, why don't we just have a peanut butter sandwich? I know you are tired of cooking." Actually, he was tired of turning the oven on and off.

"Oh, dinner. Why, yes, dinner. Are you hungry?"

Really, I wasn't. I'd passed my hungry time.

When I was finally pain-free, I found I had lost 10 pounds. I was so grateful that I wrote him a letter of thanks for those meals and his help.

And then I left for Paris and Maxim's for a weeklong pig-out.

Don't Phase Me Out

Having one of your children, especially a 21-year-old, home with the flu isn't the fun and games that it used to be when he was younger.

When he was a small boy and was home sick from school, there was a natural maternal nursing pattern. I flapped my wings around him like a mother hen. We'd have orange juice every two hours. We'd look at "Captain Kangaroo" together, and "Father Knows Best." We'd play cards, tic-tac-toe, and I'd read "Charlotte's Web" to him. I'd ask the patient, "Do you want an eating surprise or a toy surprise?" before heading for the market.

He'd say, "Either, Mom," his feverish eyes lighting up with pleasure.

I'd sit by his bed and we'd tell ghost stories and sip hot chocolate.

Now I can't sit on the bed anymore because there are tapes and records all over it mixed with college textbooks.

So these kids grow up into men and women with minds and bodies of their own. And you try to cut the umbilical cord that turns into a long telephone cord, which you'd like to cut, too. Ever try to chain a 21-year-old to his bed when he is sick?

"The doctor says you have to stay in bed 24 hours."

"Mom, I have a final exam. I have to get up soon. My fever is down. I can feel it." Then he closes his eyes, puts his earphones on and sleeps. No, he doesn't want orange juice, and he doesn't even want to do "knock-knock" jokes together.

Later, he asks if I happen to have on hand a loaf of Italian bread, brie cheese and a bottle of wine. I make him vegetable soup. He leaves all the peas in the plate. He tells me if Dixie or Mary call, wake him immediately.

But in general, I realize I've been phased out as a mother.

I bring him his pills. He says, "Just put them there and I will take them later. I'm a big boy, Mom, but wait, Mom, will you read this crazy thermometer for me before you go."

"It says 100 degrees," I announce triumphantly. Then I leave the room with a resigned sigh to go find the cat to mother. But I lock his door on the way out. As weak as he is, it will take him a while to pick the lock.

A Diary of the Flu

I had the flu and it was fun — for a little while, anyway. Here's a diary of how it went.

THE FIRST DAY — I was served breakfast in bed, pancakes, complete with a yellow plastic rose on the tray. Lunch, too, a peanut butter sandwich served on a cookie sheet. It was the first peanut butter sandwich I could remember eating and not having made myself.

When dinner time arrived, the family debated whether to allow me to come to the table. First, they took my temperature. It was 101, so I got another meal in bed — a turkey TV dinner.

Later, our youngest child insisted on bringing me fresh hot-water bottles every hour. The evening was almost cozy. I felt like a queen.

THE SECOND DAY — The service dropped off. Mommy in bed no longer qualified as a novelty. In addition, I had started coughing. They were afraid I was spreading germs.

My temperature had dropped to a mere 100, and I no longer received full family benefits. No breakfast in bed or lunch or dinner. In fact, I never did get lunch.

As for dinner, they didn't consult me. I "dropped by" the kitchen to see what they were making. The selection was chili tuna. I had tea and toast.

THE THIRD DAY — I was up and around. I cleaned out the refrigerator and washed all 42 glasses and the eight pounds of silverware the family had left me. Thank God they had used paper plates.

I felt reasonably well. I got dressed to go out. Then it happened!

He called, "Honey, I feel awful. I must have caught your flu. I'm coming home early from the office. Turn down the bed. Get the hot-water bottle. Call the doctor. I'm much sicker than you were."

"OK," I replied. "I'll get out the plastic rose."

"Don't be funny," he snapped.

I got out the rose and then lay down on the couch. I felt awful again. I'd had a relapse.

Chapter 18

Buy One, Get One for Me

Her Moves Are Marvelous

One crying baby doll.
Two empty gerbil cages.
Three damaged hair dryers.
Four bottomless rain coats.
Five golden rings (tarnished wedding bands).

These items are just part of Bobo Schwartz's haul this month. Bobo is a friend of mine whose moves are a marvel at stores that have special sales every few minutes at different counters.

No dash from counter to counter is too long in her quest for the Great Buy — even if she doesn't need the particular item on sale.

Yesterday, she went to a classic storewide, closeout sale that had interval sales every 15 minutes.

She said it took her all day long even on roller skates, getting from one counter to another, and three hours extra to check out.

Her specialty is not without risks. At many stores, the wages of women moving to and fro can have a steamroller effect, crushing toes and shopping carts alike.

"Bobo, what's your secret?" I wanted to know.

A keen ear focused on the loudspeaker, she explained.

"A voice comes over the store's public address system. The red flag is up at the sporting goods counter, and for the next 15 minutes you can get our fabulous name brand tennis shoes for $1 a pair.' Then I'm off."

Bobo racked up 15 pairs.

Then, "Ladies, the red flag is up at the cloth counter. You may purchase

10 yards of our quality fabric for just $2."

Bobo brought 30 yards and doesn't sew.

Or "Housewives, we have 16-ounce jars of Pennsylvania Peanuts for 25 cents, so hurry to the red flag counter."

And "The red flag is up at gloves. These are genuine leather, imported from Eastern Punjab, for $2."

She bought a dozen pair.

"Now hear this, ladies! We have 100 mismatched men's socks at 5 cents. Hurry, hurry."

All day long Bobo hurried.

"Bobo," I said, "why, why, why?"

"Did you actually save money? In other words, you spent about $100 yesterday and $5 worth of gasoline getting there, and those tennis rackets you bought don't have any strings. I mean, did you get anything that you really needed?"

"Of course not, I just buy at random for random."

"Wait a minute," I said. "What is 'random'?"

"'Random' is all my friends and family who at some time might need a jar of peanuts, size 13 AAA tennis shoes, a crib mattress — and as for the raincoats, they can sew their own buttons on."

Male Shoppers: Quick and Often Wrong

It all started in a local department store. I was looking at mini-slips at the lingerie counter (I used to call it underwear until I moved to a big city) when I overheard the clerk say, "Do you want something filmy or tailored, sir?" And then, sir said, "I want something I can see through, but no one else can" (lecherous laughter from sir).

I suddenly realized it was really Christmas time, and the menfolk were out shopping. A naturally curious type, I asked the clerk if many men bought underwear, pardon me, lingerie, at Christmas time.

Wow. She confessed a bunch of things that are fit to print.

She said that more single men buy lingerie for their girlfriends than married men for their wives. (How does that grab you, Mrs. Housewife?)

"Would you believe," she said, "that a man bought a black girdle with a red zipper the other day. He told me his girl wore a size 10 shoe and 7 glove, that was all I had to go on.

"Four days later, he was back with the girdle. His girl was furious as it was three sizes too big, and it broke up their engagement."

She said that most men brought with them lists of sizes. "Lingerie is a pretty tricky affair." That was the understatement of the late 20th century.

She told me a man had written on the back of a match box "42-25-32." So they selected comparable sizes, a size 42 bra, 32 slip and size 5 pants. What happened? The order was wrong. The woman's measurements were 32-25-42.

But the size 42-hipped woman was pretty nice about the exchange, the clerk told me. She told the saleslady she was bringing the lingerie back because it was all the wrong color — she didn't like pink.

But if the lingerie clerk had some stories, the lady who sells the wigs was positively garrulous. She told me that many men are buying their wives wigs or wig certificates. She lowered her voice to tell me about the man who clipped off a piece of his wife's hair while she was sleeping and brought it in to match for a wig.

But most of the clerks I talked to told me that men are much nicer to wait on at Christmas time. They are more polite, spend more money and don't haggle. They just make quick and wrong decisions.

Now, the way I feel, I'd rather him blunder in the lingerie department than give me a new vacuum cleaner.

My neighbor has the right idea; she just gets all her appliances fixed before Christmas, so he won't surprise her with something utilitarian. In the past, she has received for Christmas a washer for the kitchen faucet, an extension cord for her telephone, plastic garbage cans, a new handle for her old skillet and a box of new garters for her old girdles.

I say if you have not hinted as far back as August, you're kaput. If you have not said, "Gee, we won't be able to go to the Browns' open house because I don't have the right coat to wear over the red crepe," or "Remember Ellen Frost's pantsuit last week, wasn't that good looking?" (He remembered Ellen but not her outfit.)

I remember the Christmas I asked for a beaded evening purse and got snow tires! So this Christmas I'm asking for snow tires, just in case.

I remember when we lived in Texas, a wealthy rancher's wife told a television interviewer that she had everything she wanted. ... She needed nothing for Christmas: "I have pearls, diamonds, a mink coat; why I don't even want another oil well." Do you know what her husband gave her that year? A tax lawyer. But the trouble was she kept him. The lawyer, that is.

Sunday Morning at the Drive-in Flea Market

"Get it here, get it here, I don't take pesos, but get it here, get your carved trays from Mexico here. ..."

The guy's in some kind of weird getup. If I met him on the sidewalk, I would cross the street. He has a wide-brimmed sombrero with feathers hanging from it. He's in a T-shirt and polyester pants with a lamb's wool vest. His hair is in a ponytail.

But he's just one of the many hawkers at a local flea market. And no, he's not selling fleas. But he is dancing up and down, sort of like a flea, though that's not why they call this carnival of stuff a flea market.

The flea market is a hand-me-down idea from European outdoor markets. You might say people sell some things that look like they might be flea-ridden (although I don't mean to cast aspersions on your great-grandmother's antimacassars).

Webster says a flea market is a market where inexpensive or secondhand items are for sale.

Well, Webster would be turning over in his grave because now flea markets have anything from new and expensive items to antiques, old clothing, comic books and lots of plain, old junk.

So let me get my secondhand oar in. I went to my first large flea market recently. In fact, I went in place of church, and believe me I didn't hear any bells. But I heard lots of cash registers ringing that good, old American tune — "capitalism and ingenuity go hand in hand." The market was at a drive-in movie theater.

No one was singing hymns, either, but lots of people were whistling, 'cause they'd just ripped off someone by selling sunglasses for $5 that cost them $2.

There were hundreds of customers and about 350 stalls. You have to rent the stalls, and you pay a minimum to get in. But it's worth it. Where else can you get rid of your moth-eaten postcard collection or old coat hangers?

In the course of one day, a "flea" spokesman told me, about 6,000 people wander through. In fact, the drive-in makes more money on the flea markets than on its movies.

What fascinated me was not just what people were selling — and believe me, there were some good bargains — but what people were wearing.

The dress code was somewhere between the Fourth of July at Jones Beach and a busy evening in Casablanca.

It was hot, and that is the kind of weather that "flea-ers" like. There were halters and shorts on women. There was a woman in white gloves. And there were men in cutoffs. There was a man in a red silk jump suit with a sailor's cap and a man sweating in a three-piece suit.

If you are looking for an octagonal glass door knob or a wooden toilet seat, it's here.

In fact, flea markets seem to be a haven for hard-core hardware nuts. The hardware stalls are the most popular. And if you are looking for a used typewriter or a carved duck, this is your place. But you do have to remember that the typewriter can turn into a lemon and the duck a turkey. There's no guarantee.

I think the crowds at a flea market show two things: People are poorer than 10 years ago, so they are looking for bargains, and they also have learned that if you put a piece of junk on a counter with other pieces of junk, and yell, "Get it here," someone will.

And listen, don't feel bad about going to a flea market instead of to church. At least you aren't out in the sunshine playing golf and indulging yourself. Right?

Fairy Tells New Tale

Once upon a time there was a fairy. She was called the secondhand fairy, because she lived underneath the root of a giant oak tree. Her whole house was furnished with secondhand things that humans had lost or thrown out.

The fairy didn't throw away anything. Her bathtub was a silver thimble, her baby's playpen was an old wedding band and her clothesline was an old shoestring, her bed a match box.

Maybe you remember that fairy tale. I do, because I know a secondhand fairy. She's my neighbor, Molly.

Molly doesn't live under the root of a tree, but I'll bet her husband wishes that she did. Molly is a second hand nut.

I mean, she is a collector. She never throws anything out. She has all her second-grade arithmetic papers in a carton. She has a small box that holds her great-grandfather's bridge work — he's dead now. She has 16 World War II ration books. She has more old papers in her attic than the Library of Congress.

Oh, yes, she has a ball of twine that is so large now they have to keep it out in the cactus garden.

I talked Molly into a garage sale. They are a weekend pastime that has become more popular than baseball, football and the builders' "open houses." It's a new game for indiscriminating adults, and you don't have to dress up.

I secretly think Molly has been going by "tag" sales without me, so she could have a giant sale of her own. I mean, where did she get the pocketbook made from old cigarette packages?

Our sale was a big success, because our husbands went fishing and our kids sold snow cones. We had a stereo speaker hooked up outside and Molly's chihuahua tied up outside, in case of shoplifters. We were very professional.

The purpose of the sale was to clean out Molly's garage so that her kids could use it as a pool hall, but what really happened was she sold her garage.

I sold three sick geranium plants for 5 cents, one playpen that didn't fold for $2, four pastry cutters that we got for wedding presents (but I can't make pastry that you can cut), three shopping bags with Best and Company marked on them for 2 cents, two used electric light bulbs for 10 cents, a pair of ski boots (but one was a size 10 and the other was a size 8) for $2, one man's tie with a cigarette burn and six battle ribbons from World War I.

I made just enough money to pay for the flavors for the making of the snow cones.

As a matter of fact, I tagged one 3-year-old who was running around with a sale tag marked "bargain at $25." Do you know no one bought him?

Oh yes, Molly's husband had a brand new grill and we put it out with my new cookbook on "How to Prepare Crepe Suzettes" (these items were what you call "come-ons" to make people really think we had top-rate items), and guess what? Molly sold that grill before her husband came home for $45. He only paid $12.50 for it.

I'll tell you what, though, Molly is still a secondhand fairy. She made $100 at the sale, and with that money she bought a secondhand desk with millions of little drawers to store millions of little things that humans discard.

Chapter 19

The *Later Dater*

Maudlin Martyrs' Club

Joan is a member of the Maudlin Martyrs' Club. It's almost a secret society, because if you are part of it, you don't know you are in it and you don't pay dues.

Actually, I've known many MMs in my lifetime. I've even helped maudlin martyrs by giving them too much sympathy, which is what they want more than anything.

No, I'm not talking Joan of Arc — a true martyr; I'm talking ordinary women, usually over middle age. And I presume more women have this complex than men. Men don't like to be seen crying, wringing their hands or appearing less macho. However, I'm sure at bars many a man has unburdened his woes to the bartender.

First, let me explain that whining is different from being a maudlin martyr. Martyrs want to be applauded, put on a pedestal.

Joan is a "House-Maven Martyr." She wants praise for all she does, She wants someone to say. "How do you do it all?" or simply, "You are the most."

Joan wants compliments for the curtains she made and the jellies she canned and the laundered aluminum foil she reuses. Applause, applause, she craves it.

She maintains that she never gets through. She cleans with a Q-tip, and her grandchildren exhaust her. Heading her complaint list is, "Why do I always have to cook the holiday dinners?" Blah, blah, blah. She can't suffer enough.

But worse than Joan is Mildred. She is a "Never-Have-Enough-Money Martyr." "We never travel. We can't afford it. He retired too soon. I've never been anywhere. These are supposed to be our golden years, instead they are our tarnished years." I told her one day I know women who have never left their own city, but she didn't believe me.

One of the most self-deprecating types is the "Club-Lady Martyr." Every time

I see her, she has just swept out the clubhouse, mended the curtains in the parish hall or she has made dozens of meat loaves for the end-of-the-year dinner. What she does accomplish in the community is negated by the gripes about her work. She bellyaches about all the good she is spreading in her community; therefore, let's stop giving her applause and just say, "thank you." I have told her that I'm sure the Lord loveth a cheerful giver. But she isn't.

There is the "Nine-to-Five Martyr" who can't quit her job because she loves to complain about it. She tells me that her boss is terrible and her husband doesn't help at home, and she has a scowl on her face every time I see her.

The martyr complex can run deep. My Aunt Sarah had a bad case of it, from "I have terrible hair" to "I'm too fat" to "I'm miserable" to "my new teeth never fit." A year after her husband died, she married a great guy, and her troubles and complaints disappeared. No, she didn't grow new teeth, she just adhered to the old adage, "My glass is half-full, not half-empty."

The ultimate in martyrs is the "I-Am-Sicker-Than-You Martyr." For an hour, she can list her ailments and discomforts in rapid fire. You can't beat her litany of new knee replacement surgery and joint aches.

Ann Landers often talks about the martyr complex and that some people truly need counscling, as in the case of the young girl who had to take in her sick mother and care for her four kids in a small house.

This column is not to denigrate the real, true-blue people who constantly help others without reward or discourse. But the Maudlin Martyrs I know could form their own "Sympathy Seekers Symphony." They are out there loud and clear. Hear them roar.

Caught in the Middle

They call them the "sandwich generation" — meaning that they are caught between two categories or two worlds.

Somewhere around the age of 40 to 50, they are taking care of their kids, plus their aging parents. Many of the couples are two-parents-working families.

Different from the 1950s when not as many women were in the workplace, these couples find it a struggle to be caretakers of both generations. Statistics tell us that people are living longer, and this means the "sandwiched couples" have a dual and heavier load.

I hear them griping about their daily lives — that they are stressed out all the time and that they are working harder than ever before while taking care of so many members of their family. Many feel besieged, they say.

In fact, some social scientists say that they — the baby boomers — are a generation of privilege raised by a generation of people who sacrificed. And that the sandwich-filling parents usually went to college, and, therefore, have more education than former generations.

Well, I don't want to be a critic here. Instead, I want to laud those who are still raising kids or sending them to college while they take care of their own aging parents.

I think they are going to get through this stage of their lives, because they are better educated than ever. Also, most of them love their families and don't want to let anybody down.

In my own family, for example, my son, a scientist, and his wife, a teaching lawyer, equally divide all their house and domestic work. The one who gets home first fixes dinner; the one who is free on Saturday morning does the laundry. I have seen each one cook a gourmet meal and help their daughter with her homework. They also make frequent trips to Florida to check on her stroke-ridden father and caretaker mother.

I have neighbors with four children, both the mother and father work and they take care of an Alzheimer's parent in their house. They made their garage into an apartment.

I also have a friend of 38 who stays home with his children, 3 and 5, in the daytime, while his wife teaches during the day. When she comes home he goes off to work, as a night reporter for a paper. The father is indeed a Mr. Mom, and does it well. In their one guest room is his mother, who broke her hip and is 75.

In fact, most of the young men I know between 30 and 50 know how to market, cook and change a baby's diaper. They are a new genre of men. My father did not go into the kitchen, and my husband never did laundry or changed a baby's diaper.

So if the sandwich-filling 50-year-olds are stressed, I think they can take it. They are smart, ingenious and expect a lot of themselves. I see a generation who will survive their hardships, just as our generation lived through World War II with strength and sacrifice. I want to pay tribute to the young husband or wife who can take care of a baby and have a career, too. Their generation is savvy and has lots of energy and love for their kids and their parents.

One young girl said, about having her mother live with them, "We feel it is great that my kids can see old age up close and know what it is going to be like to grow old. We like our mother living with us. Sure, there are rules — as every family has to have rules — and all ages must abide by them."

And then recently I asked a 50ish woman what she likes about having so many generations under one roof, and she told me, "You do what you have to do," then she smiled.

That's it for all of us, isn't it?

The Bridge over Troubled Waters

Bridge has always eluded me, and now it's time to buckle down and learn to play.

At least that is what some of my friends are saying. "Look, you don't have a job, you are retired and you aren't getting any younger — play," they tell me. (These are friends?)

However, there are about three of my friends who have said, "Well, Elise, you don't remember where you parked the car at Towsontown Mall, how are you going to remember your cards?"

They are all right.

A neighbor called to warn me that bridge is "concentration and communication." Well, I can communicate. So perhaps it's time to try it one more time and hunker down to the rudiments of this famous game.

I think what I will like about bridge is the gossip.

I overhear people playing bridge in clubs, in senior centers, in houses, everywhere, and they all seem to be laughing and having a very good time. Or is it just that I feel like I'm on the outside looking in?

Gossip is not mean if it's therapeutic, right? And think how boring your day would be without one tiny bit of gossip. Or maybe we'd feel better about it if we called it "trivial news."

The other thing I would like about the bridge brigade is the terrific food — cheese puffs, appetizers and desserts. One bridge hostess served trifle pudding around Christmas and last month, she made creme brulee. I have tried to horn in on the eating part of a bridge party, but I guess that is rude — going to the bridge game, gossiping and eating but not having a bridge hand. Not de rigueur, huh?

Right now, I'm conducting my own survey: Does playing bridge make women gain weight? Especially in the derriere? I'll report it in two years.

Anyway, about every five years or so, I have written about how I'm going to learn to play bridge. After all, my 9-year-old grandson can play chess. Certainly I can master this popular sitting-down sport.

So the other day I went to a senior center to see when I could start bridge classes. It was semester break. The teacher, with a deep, wide frown, said, "Oh, no, I don't take beginners. Haven't you played at all?"

Oh yes, I played bridge once in San Diego in 1943 under a blackout light in a hotel room with three other Navy wives.

After that, I sought other venues to learn — places that might want me. One teacher asked me, "Well, what do you do for fun, if you don't play bridge?" "Oh, my," I told her, "let me count the ways." I found myself explaining my spare time since 1924; there wasn't much spare.

Now, I want to strike back at all those devotees. Listen, by the time you play bridge for four hours, I've read two books.

The amazing thing is that bridge is coming back BIG in spite of Walkmans, television and home videos. They say that 20 million people still play bridge. Darn it, I want to be counted!

Now you can play it on your computer. The Internet is attracting many new people. There are over 600 bridge-related Web sites. They call it the New Deal. Cool.

Bridge is full of off-color lingo like trumps, rubbers, partners and tricks. I have wondered what "two no trump" really means. And now I want to know because the only trump I know is Donald. Turning a trick is not the same as winning one in bridge. I understand in bridge you can be a dummy and not feel dumb. Great.

If I don't learn bridge soon, I will switch to chess. My 8-year-old neighbor says she will teach me, and my grandson is standing by to give Gran basic training in chess. So, there, I will get back at my bridge addicts.

But my grandson has reminded me, "If you play chess, Gran, you can't gossip, and you can't eat."

Ah, shucks.

Saluting a Generation

I just finished reading Tom Brokaw's new book, "The Greatest Generation."

Were we? Maybe.

I was there. Were you? If you were, you will enjoy this major memoir. There are pictures and sketches of the ordinary men and women and famous people — all heroes who participated in the ethic of World War II.

Brokaw also highlights the women, which makes that war seem all the more historic and valiant.

What I read made me look back. I don't usually remind myself of the war years. Perhaps because they took a slice of life out of our early marriage and our lives. My husband was on active Navy duty for five years, and all the battles do not bring back fond memories for me of that global struggle. Most of the heroes in the book came of age during the Depression and then went on to build a resolute America.

Brokaw writes that the men and women born a few years on either side of 1920 made up the greatest generation any society has produced. And he tells why he thinks so.

The book makes good reading. Among the pages I found many types of fine people I came to know during those years — and they and their value systems are worth lauding

Reading the book, I realized that my four children and five grandchildren never asked me about that war.

Now we talk of the Civil War; it has come back in style. We talk of the unpopular war — Vietnam — and we talk of the Gulf War and the present trouble with Iraq. But World War II, other than old Jimmy Stewart movies and the 1998 blockbuster movie "Saving Private Ryan," seems like a bad dream to the generation of baby boomers that follows us into the 1990s and the millennium.

Looking back, I feel we were very brave. From saying goodbye to the ones we loved to rationing and shortages — canned food, no meat — to playing cards under blackout lights, we learned about deprivation.

Mostly loneliness and fear permeated our everyday existence. Our mantra word was "peace," praying for the end of conflict.

Maybe our children will read this and find out why we did it and how we did it.

Brokaw, who interviews many who are still alive, today, writes of the spiritual belief that helped the front-liners cope with possible death, serious injuries and other anxieties. I believe that. He has documented some 50 Americans, some you will recognize — former Oregon Sen. Mark Hatfield, George Bush, Sen. Daniel Inouye of Hawaii, Joe Foss, a famed Marine fighter pilot, then later governor of South Dakota, and Gen. Jeanne Holm, whose distinguished military career includes NATO, Vietnam and back to Washington as a consultant. The writer delves into their backgrounds and their raison d'etre.

What did I notice in this book? That there is a commonality that runs through each chapter — inherent bravery and intrepid spirit.

Today, I see friends who are sick with incurable diseases, infirmities or who are dying practicing that wartime courage. I have wondered how or why they are so indomitable. I think former Gov. Joe Foss, now in his 80s, answered that question. He told Brokaw at the end of the interview, "Those of us who live have to represent those who didn't make it."

And as you will read, the other golden thread that runs through is faith that seems inculcated in their lives — then and now.

The author states that those men and women forged the values and provided the training that made a people and a nation great. Their courage gives us the world we have today. Yet this book is no intellectual tome — it is simply a salute that reads easily. Tom Brokaw has made us sit up, look back and applaud.

The Later Dater

"Dear Ann Landers, no, wait ... I mean, Dear Dr. Joyce Brothers, have you written a book about dating at 70-something?" No, well then, I wish you would.

I guess I never imagined I'd live to be dating "later." Yes, that's right, it can happen, especially if you are lonely, aren't married anymore (as in divorced or widowed) or don't have a dog to keep you company.

I don't want this to be too personal, so don't call unless you own a Lear jet, yacht or Greek island and are divorced or widowed and over 60. This is not a dating ploy. In fact, I find the company of women much more relaxing, because there are no social rules. Like, should I call him if I've only gone out with him once? Should I "ex" him out of my files if he has ever done computer dating or has never been married?

I just want to whine about how difficult it is to be "dating." You see, I had not dated a man since I dated my late husband in 1943, and then, smack, right away, I married him.

So here goes. First of all, as you know, women outlive men, so there aren't that many fish in the sea. That's an expression my mother used when my sister or I were disappointed in a friend or actually were ditched by some stupid boy — "Well, dear, there are more fish in the sea."

The trouble is that now I don't know what sea is out there and how rough it is. Men that are free, as in available, are either too fat, too thin, too sick, too shy, too old, too young, or want to get married so there will be someone at the helm to cook, clean and iron shirts for them.

Before I go any further, I want you to know that I have had some dates in the past few years. Oh, yeah, I'm not desperate. I don't ask the dinner-time telemarketers how old they are when they call.

Now, I have a bunch of questions for Ann Landers or Dr. Joyce Brothers. When a man asks us out, do we say, "That's great, what time?" Or do you tell him what time or "some" time? Or do we play hard-to-get — "I may be in Fiji, call me next year." (That will give you time to look up his past.)

Then, on the first date, do you ask him into the front parlor to meet mother, like you did when you were 16? (But my mother's been dead 33 years.) Or do you introduce him to your divorced son who just moved back in and is lounging around the living room? A dog is nice to introduce him to. You can tell a lot about a man in how he looks at or pets your dog. If the new date overdoes it, and plays with Fido and snatches away the dog's rubber bone, forget him; he's controlling. If he doesn't touch the dog, listen carefully about his childhood experiences with dogs and cats.

Then do you make your date sit if he's 70 or 80, while you go comb your hair again and get your purse? Or do you get your own coat and hand it to him? Or do you put on your own coat? Do you open the car door and jump in, or do you let him open the car door? Or do you suggest you meet him at the pub, restaurant or movie for the first date?

Do you ask him in for a drink before you go out? Watch for this as he may be so nervous, and you are, too, that he will want a drink. This be a way to find out if he's in AA or is a current big boozer.

Do you ask him in after the date, and for what? And be careful here as he may not like chocolate chip cookies and milk? Remember you are not 16. If he tries to kiss you on the first date, forget him, but keep him on file.

Seriously, some of these questions are answered in a brand new book by Dr. John Gray, "Mars and Venus, Starting Over." He is the author of the best seller "Men are from Mars, Women are from Venus, A Practical Guide to Finding Love Again After a Loss." At one point he suggests, "A woman needs to date three men during the same time frame." Wow!

Oh, the questions we could ask Joyce Brothers and Ann Landers.

Here are a few pertinent things to find out. If he has taken you out for dinner, say five times, shouldn't you take him out to dinner next? After all, when we were young, most boys asked me to meet them inside the theater, but back then no one had any money. Another widow tells me she and her man go "Dutch." The only trouble is they can't remember who paid last.

I have a friend who is very rational at 70 and is dating a 40-year-old man. They are having a great time and plan to marry. She's had a face-lift and a tummy tuck, she looks super now. But when he is 70, she will be 100 and may be irrational or, worse, dead. And that sounds so risky and scary to me.

I'll Take My September at the Beach

You may call August the "dog days of summer," but I believe the real dog days are September. For me, September is a blight on the calendar.

You may remember "September Song." It went something like, "Oh, it's a long, long while from May to December, but the days go short when you reach September," blah blah, then, "When autumn leaves fall, the days settle down to a precious few ... those precious days I will spend with you."

Oh, they can make a sad love song out of anything. But my recollections of Septembers are not romantic. They are "just get me through this stupid month and get onto the better weather and hopefully exciting routines of daily life."

First of all, September is too hot or too cold. It doesn't know what it is itself. You don't know what to wear. Are white shoes still good in September at 90 degrees? Are black bags OK then? And there's no special food for September — corn and hot dogs are old stuff.

Seriously, I have never liked the month because it reminds me of changes and goodbyes — neither of which I really like.

As far as city activities, they seem to be on hold. In September, you wait for things to change. The pools are vacant, the streets are not alive with the sound of any kind of music, the ice cream man with the truck has gone and the school buses roll.

It was always the month when my four kids left for school, sometimes a new school, bringing on new angst and queasiness. With small children and first grade, you give up most of your parenthood and directorship for the time they will spend with a new teacher and new friends. The youngsters become different somehow.

Then there was the leave-for-college time. What are they getting into?

Will they like it enough to stay there? Why do their voices seem louder? The anticipation of another world, a new experience. I was often scared for them.

Unlike many mothers who couldn't wait for their kids to get out of their hair, I could wait. I missed them when they left, with their new shoes and school bags. I missed them even when I had a job I loved. I missed the doors slamming, the telephone ringing, the sweet moments of real communication between mother and child. I got them off with lots of kisses, hugs and admonitions. I would smile, but the smile was a little hollow.

In September, I get a deep longing, even now. Not a depression, but a longing — I know not why. For what? For where? For whom? For more children running around the house? For a new adventure for myself? A cruise, a trip across the world? A malaise of some sort sets in.

September also means that the evenings will be darker. Daylight saving time will come upon us soon. Maybe the body clock changes in September. I spent some time in Southern California one year during World War II, and there was no change in climate in September. That, too, was strange. A solstice link seemed to be missing.

But wait, I do find solace in September at the ocean. The beach on the East Coast is supreme in September, and the water is still warm. The sunset still spreads its fiery tentacles over the bay, and the sunrise still brings a splendid promise. And the boardwalk has slowed its summer frenzy.

As I walk along the beach and let my toes touch the white foam of the tide, my soul regenerates, my spirit lifts. Even the shells seem different. There are fewer, as there are fewer human footprints on the wet sand. Ah, but with the first big storm of the solstice, the shells will reappear.

The seagulls are fewer. They miss the people's scraps — the chips and fries. Then suddenly for our pleasure, a formation of huge birds flies over. They are going south. Cormorants? Ducks?

September at the beach is still the thunder of the waves, and we know they are everlasting and mysterious.

The Talking Car

I want to talk about "The Talking Car." No, not the high-tech cars that electronically talk to you and have synthesized voice systems.

I mean the car trips or rides that enable a parent and child to converse without any interruptions. When you just use the ride time for a good talk.

Whether a child is 4-years-old or 40-years-old, when that child and a parent get in a car together, they are unencumbered by television or other people's voices. They can talk. A car also enables husband and wife to converse on a trip without the kids listening or interjecting bad behavior.

Maybe that's one reason I like my car so much — it has afforded me privacy. When the kids were growing up, it was a vehicle for bonding and/or complaints that I would not have heard at the dining room table.

When the children were living at home, especially when they were teenagers, my husband and I had our best communication times in the car together — driving somewhere. Maybe it's because we both loved driving and we knew we were not being overheard by our four children.

I can remember times when I asked my husband to take me for a long car ride so I could explain one of the children's immediate problems to him, directly and in-depth.

I miss the encapsulated, cloud-like feeling the car gave us while driving a child to and from school. There was an unusual intimacy when parent and child converse sitting next to one another. I relaxed and felt the child's innermost self was surrounding me like a warm quilt. And we could unravel any intimate problems. Together, alone.

I remember taking each child at a certain time in his or her life for a ride in the car to tell him or her the facts of life. I think my husband was meant to "do" the boys and I was meant to inform the girls, but I found I did both.

With no eye contact in the front seat, I felt freer and the child felt less self-conscious with this exchange.

I remember a year when one of the girls was 10 and I had to tell her that my mother, her grandmother, who was visiting at that time, had just died. I picked up my child to bring her home, so she would not get on the usual school bus. I needed her to myself. So I drove around for a while and told her about mother's death, then we went to get an ice cream cone. I parked, we discussed death and, at last, we hugged and cried.

In fact, to back me up on the theory of one-to-one talking relationships, the *Journal of the American Medical Association* recently announced, as a result of the largest survey ever done of adolescent health in the United States, that kids need to talk and we need to listen more. Also, the survey showed that children are really acutely tuned in to their parents' opinions, contrary to what we sometimes think.

The *Journal* emphasized that strong emotional connections with parents are a key in helping teen-agers avoid high-risk behavior.

I would like to add for those of us who have grandchildren and drive them places that here again a car is often a cozy, enclosed space for listening and talking. Remember there are more grandparents alive today than ever before, so we can help interact.

I have had very revealing conversations with my grandchildren in the car. A 9-year-old asked me, "Should Mom and Dad have another baby?" I said that I thought it was up to them. She thought it was up to her to decide, so we worked that subject over for about half an hour.

And cars are amazing, too. Driving with a child over the whir of the traffic, you may hear the whir of a young heart that is unfolding. For you.

Perchance to Sleep

We were sitting around a neighbor's den. Just old friends visiting after dinner. We were all over 65, I'm more than sure, although Ilsa never tells how old she is. We actually don't talk about our age anymore.

Let's see, there were three couples and then a bunch of widows. Remember, women outlive men, even in our kind and gentle neighborhood. It's a place where there are more people over 60 than under 30. My neighbors have aged like their siding — slowly, gracefully, but with some visible changes.

We have all known one another for as long as we've lived here, which makes for mature gossip. It's less vehement and is less about on-the-job politics now because we are all retired.

We had finished complaining or bragging about our grandchildren when we got started talking about a weird subject. And I'm reporting in.

I guess because we are older, by now we all have strange built-in methods of sleeping. I'm not talking about sex or recreation. I'm talking about adults who, like babies, have to sleep in certain positions to have a good night's sleep.

One burly, athletic man, who was a former coach, said he had to have a baby pillow under his neck when he sleeps on his right side. It is a pillow he had as a child, and he takes it or, rather, sneaks it into his carry-on luggage when he travels.

Julia, a lovely normal woman of 70, has to have a light on to go to sleep. Her husband has to wear eye shades to cut out the light so he can sleep. They both admit if they can't sleep by 2 in the morning they get up and play cribbage.

Betty Sue, who grew up in a family with six girls, has to have the battery-radio plugs in her ears to nod off.

I am happy to report that the men reported more idiosyncrasies in sleep habits than the women did.

Chuck has to have his feet free of sheets at the bottom of the bed, and when he goes to a motel or hotel, he has to undo the sheets so he can sleep bare-toed. Another man admitted to that. And one confessed he still slept naked — like a baby.

And yes, before your ask, all of the couples still sleep in the same bed. Two of the bad back-people have to sleep on their sides with a pillow between their knees, not unusual. But it was strange to hear what types of pillows are used.

John uses a small pillow and, according to his wife, she had to sew Velcro on the pillow so it would stick to his hairy knees when he turns. Millie, on the other hand, uses a small plastic sack filled with leaves.

Now I could tell you some other secrets, even though I've changed the names and the venue. But I think it is too mean to tell of one guy who sleeps on his back and has to have the pillow over his face. Tom has to have a fan on to lull him to sleep, even in winter, and all the closet doors in their big bedroom have to be closed.

Me, I sleep well as long as I can grab the open end of the pillowcase and twist it between my fingers.

Look, I know bad-back people shouldn't sleep on their stomach, but I found that there were quite a few women sleeping on their stomach still.

Mary sleeps on her left side always, because she is convinced it bodes better for the pumping of her heart

OK, I have never gone to a sleep clinic, but I can tell all of you who are over 60, if you aren't taking a prescribed sleeping pill or Tylenol PM, you are welcome to try any of the above methods of sleeping.

Easy Marks

This is a trilogy of sorts, three examples of how women alone are too vulnerable.

Do older women who live alone get ripped off? I think so.

Betsy called two months ago and told me she'd hired a man to rebuild her back porch. He had been recommended by a neighbor, a friend. Betsy lives on a fixed income, but wants to keep the house up to par. She figured she could afford the work.

He quoted her $7,000. That seemed fair, so she didn't get another bid. OK? Not OK. That was her first mistake.

He started before October when the weather was good and said he'd have it done in two weeks — his first mistake. She gave him a check for $3,000 down as be requested. The rest was due when the job was finished.

He did not start when he said he would. When he did start, he forgot to put in a new door. And the windows he ordered were too small and not according to his meager sketch. He told her he was saving her some money by using windows left over from another job. When the final bill came, it was twice the original price.

A new widow, she missed talking over the deal with her husband who knew a little more than she did about carpentry work. She said her husband would have been firmer and more demanding. Sure, women are born to be the supplicant and appeasers. Women of my generation weren't born to be warriors with tradesmen.

Then the contractor told her he couldn't finish it until the weather got better. He hadn't figured in the paint job, so that was extra. By December, the porch was half-finished and the new roof leaked and the doors were not put in correctly. She is taking him to court, maybe.

Next in our trilogy is Mary Sue and the field of dentistry. Recently, Mary Sue called to tell me about the dentist she went to and that he told her she needed five teeth crowned. The bill would be thousands of dollars. She told him she'd let him know, she had to talk it over with her husband, because that was a lot of money. She doesn't have a husband, but she thought that bluff would give her more leverage with the dentist. She talked it over with me, but what do I know about dentistry?

I told her to go to another dentist. "Tell him you want another opinion and probably a new dentist."

Surprise, the second dentist said she didn't have to have those teeth crowned. They were in good shape. But there was one tooth that should be resurfaced or rebuilt. It had an old filling. That would be about $75. She thanked him and signed on.

She thought that a dentist is like any other professional — until you get bids to compare, you don't know who to believe.

And then there is me and my car. Driving alone, north from Virginia, I heard the brakes squeak many times. I was in a small town, and I felt that the brakes should be looked at before I went further.

The first filling station mechanic told me I might need to have the brakes relined. So I went to a drive-in eatery and waited while he looked at the brakes.

He said I needed the brakes relined. Big bucks. I realized I needed another opinion, so I drove to the next small town, where I went to a dealer. He said I did not need to have them relined, that sometimes brakes just squeaked like that, especially in damp weather.

I got home safe and sound. Then a few days ago, I spotted a few oil drops on my driveway. I thought they might be from my car. I went to the nearest filling station, and the mechanic told me that the engine needed seals. Not satisfied with the costly bid, I went to a filling station where I knew the mechanic, and he said that I did not need that but "valve cover gaskets" for $125. We did that.

I can remember my husband never seemed to have the car trouble that I have. And if he did, he always got out of the car and observed the mechanic working on the car.

I felt, in both cases, that the man who was telling me what I needed was talking over my head on purpose, and was seeing an older woman who was in a hurry and was not very knowledgeable. A typical victim-consumer.

OK, so I'm paranoid. But lots of times I have felt that when a man talks to a supplier on a man-to-man basis, there is more honestly.

Now I have learned not to go ahead with a car diagnosis if I'm not sure. (Remember, I am not asking for elective surgery for my own body. It's for my car when I hear a burp or feel a malfunction.)

So I usually ask my young neighbor, who is studying to be a car mechanic, what he would recommend. He is very knowledgeable. He, too, thinks women are more gullible and thus, are open targets for higher prices.

OK, what is a loner to do? Wear a hard hat, dress like a man or take a course in carpentry, dentistry or car repair?

You guessed it. I have vowed to compare prices, be on the lookout for gougers. But first, I will sign up for a course in tai chi for relaxation and exercise, then I will get to the auto mechanics course after that. I will report bad deals to the Better Business Bureau or consumer watch dogs or form my own committee — "Duped Women Anonymous." Beware. Be informed.

Talking Junk Mail, Bunk Mail

I get the first month free at a weight-loss center. Just so happens right now I am too thin and am trying to gain weight. I can receive a free tune-up and lube, oil and filter for my car. I've been there, done that. Air Canada is offering a special flight to somewhere, if I buy a sofa. Have one — a sofa that is. At a tire and auto store, I can get full alignments for only 39 bucks and wiper blades for $2 off. Don't need those.

A convenience store is offering a weird deal — a ripe watermelon for $1.99 and pepperoni rolls for 23 cents off. But I have to come in on certain days. Silliest of all was a big ad telling me my checks are out of style and suggesting some angel or poker-playing dogs on my designer checks, "exclusive custom-made designs just for me [and thousands of others] at a low price."

Isn't it amazing what I can get if only I wanted any of the those wonderful items? I'm talking junk mail, bunk mail, and it comes through my mail slot like Niagara Falls, every live-long day.

OK, let me tell it all, I confess, I hate unsolicited mail — big, floppy pieces of newspaper ads inserted in my daily mail. Most of us over 50 with high cholesterol, high blood pressure, sore knees and in-need-of-replacement joints don't eat pepperoni, don't need any more furniture, and we don't know what a lube job really means.

Some mornings in my mail, I receive offers for cemetery lots. I hate that! Yes, I have that all planned, too, although I have not been there, done that. And if you're over 60, you probably don't want to think about caskets on sale either.

One reason I hate junk-bunk mail is that I have to take the large page ads to the curb, along with my newspapers, for recycling. I make three trips with this stuff!

Another reason I hate the junk-bunk mail is that it gets stuck in with the bills. Twice I've not paid a bill on time because it ended up clinging to a tabloid-type ad from a rental center.

And let's not forget the poor postal carrier, he or she has to carry that junk-bunk mail. (By the way, the post office does not like it called junk mail. It's called "business bulk mail.")

Most of the postal carriers I have talked to hate carrying all that extra paper. I called a spokesperson, the president of the Branch 176 of the National Association of Letter Carriers. He told me that 40 percent of the jobs in the postal service would not be there if there weren't any bulk business mail. He also added that bulk business mail is good for the economy.

No wonder there are more postal workers than ever before. (I, personally, have three different postmen, and I never know who they are or what time they come, but that's OK.) So I guess I'd better be careful with my complaints about what I call "bunk-junk-bulk business mail," if it makes revenue for the post office.

But not to be unfair or carried away, I must explain that people who are shut in and some older folks love to read their bulk, unsolicited mail. But just don't tell me about it. I told some older seniors the other day if they really wanted mail, I will write them postcards. I promise, if you are hungry for mail, I'll write. Now, isn't that a better deal than reading junk-bunk-bulk mail!

New York, New York

Joan is putting rather large curlers in the back of her head. Kim is putting three kinds of cream on her face. I am putting fingernail polish on my nails and toes.

What are we doing? We are preparing for bed. Great-grandchildren, do you know where your great-grandmothers are? No, they can't imagine.

There are just three of us, and we've just hit 70-years-old. We are in New York for a weekend reunion. But it is more a slumber party.

Kim, Joan and I have known one another for years. We were all young-marrieds in a small Texas town. We watched one another raise children, we watched one another go on to careers, then suddenly, like a Texas sandstorm, we all went on to better jobs and we moved away from one another. I thought of our husbands and realized that men are different than women in their friendships. They are more apt to share activities, business, golf or fishing. They do not nurture one another as we women do. Women like to share feelings. Our husbands were friends, too, which gave a great balance to our ties. We knew one another's mothers, too. And we knew our faults. But we three women hadn't seen one another in seven years.

Planning ahead for a spring fling, we were trying to recapture something — our youth, our vagaries, our self-esteem? Something. I wasn't sure in the beginning, but in the end I found out. I knew.

Jean's large curlers were going to give her a good-looking pageboy in the morning, our first day in New York City, and Kim's face has aged beautifully. And my large forehead wrinkle would be covered with thick makeup.

In our night clothes of various lengths, we did not look like college students in a dorm. We weren't even in the category of the old television sitcom "Kate and Allie." There was not a bracket in which to put us. We may have been more similar to Mary McCathy's "The Group," the best seller that told of the lasting friendship between women.

We had a few days to find ourselves and "do" New York. Instead, we found each other again.

However, each of us brought our separate baggage to the weekend.

I had lost my husband of 53 years a few months ago. It was, also, the anniversary of Kim's first child's death — some 40 years ago. And Joan and her husband were getting ready to move south after 40 years in the same place. We all brought some inner scars. Yet we knew we must adjust once again to getting older and the changes. For the few days, we needed to affirm that life past 60 and beyond is as much as an adventure as ever. We found out that this is true — in our laughter and our long talkfests. And that we could empower ourselves with new plans. We decided that we did not want to go gently into the night. We did not call ourselves old, never once.

I found out something wonderful — that love among three women who have known one another for ages can be rekindled at anytime.

It had been a long winter.

When I was raising my children, I always thought "three is a crowd," and I made sure there was not an uneven number of kids playing in my back yard. So I was surprised that three women, from different parts of the country and different political views, could cling together for as many years as we have. And for that weekend, we shared a large hotel bedroom.

Kim lives in Texas, Joan lives in Washington and I live in Baltimore.

The weather treated us to a beautiful, sunny New York day. We made plans the first night — a show, perhaps "Phantom of the Opera," and in the morning, three museums, the Metropolitan, the Museum of Modern Art, the Frick.

But when I heard we had to stand in line for things to see or do, I opted my first morning to see a dear friend I'd grown up with. She and her husband took me on a car tour of their New York. They pointed out all the New York attractions. And guess what? The places hadn't changed.

I did get to the Metropolitan on Saturday. I spent my last day in vast Central Park on a huge rock in the sun with my granddaughter, who teaches in New York, and her friend. We laughed and we talked about everything we could that someone my age can share with 20-somethings.

For just a while, on that weekend, I forgot about death, my husband's long illness, the 24-hour caretaking chores and wheelchairs. I tried to renew myself within, and I did. Being with people I love and respect and trying on their problems helped me. Yes, New York is a huge city full of too many people. But on a sunny weekend, it is a catharsis; it has incredible energy. It is both glamorous and clamorous.

I found out that deep friendship is lawless because there are no restrictions or family rules, no strings attached. We rejoiced in just affection and the long-term knowledge of one another.

For me, it was the laughter that clung to me all the way home and some. We cried a few times, especially at the church service we attended on Sunday. It was then it hit me; my weekend was about enduring loveships, not New York.

Stogies Are Not Just for Old Fogies

I can see my father right now, back in the 1930s, sitting in his green, worn armchair by the old Dayton radio, smoking his cigar. He smoked a lot of cigars, but there was a mysterious ritual to the whole thing — getting the cigar out of what he called a humidor, then clipping the end off with some funny-looking little clippers, blowing into the cigar — all before it was even lit.

It seemed it took forever. But, then, I was about 8 when I wondered why he did this, and what else was in that dank-smelling box. I remember a kind of good odor when the cigar first lit up, then later the whole room stank and that chair forever smelled of the cigar.

I think my mother only let him smoke in the evening back then. I do recall my father telling us that "a cigar a day keeps the doctor away." I knew he had that a little wrong, but it was his best defense. He lived to a ripe, old age. To me, it was a weird thing to do when he could be eating candy or reading the paper.

Maybe because I never smoked, the whole process seems useless.

Now, we run right into the 1990s and this year, in particular, cigar smoking is out of the closet or humidor. It is having a resurgence like mashed potatoes, bread pudding and meat loaf. How retro can we get?

The fad of women smoking cigars is really strange.

Look, girls, didn't we just get our mothers/ourselves off smoking cigarettes because of health reasons and weren't we proud?

And now what have we? In Dallas, I saw a stogie store for just women. The image is being stoked by skinny blondes in tight black dresses and yuppie businessmen in three-piece suits with cigars hanging from their mouths. Models are smoking, Demi is lighting up, and Whoopi is in an ad. Male celebrities, including Tom Selleck and Danny DeVito, are brandishing this new weapon. So what? Yet it seems to be the biggest fad since cappuccino and frappaccino.

My age does not seem to be stogieing. But who knows, there was Mrs. Andrew Jackson, remember — she smoked a pipe. Even columnist Art Buchwald gave up his cigar about 10 years ago.

Sure, the habit may have been handed down. My father ate scrapple and brains for breakfast sometimes, and my mother smoked cigarettes and wore a rat in her hair, but I'm not rushing out to buy anything that lights up in my mouth and isn't chocolate.

Listen out there, after I laughed my head off the other day at a 14-year-old smoking a cigar behind a schoolyard fence, I felt like dropping pamphlets from a plane on the horrors of lung diseases.

Statistics tell us that cigar bars are in and that cigars are bigger than Perrier. And that the number of women cigar smokers has doubled since 1994, up to 200,000 of the nation's 10 million cigar smokers. Natch, the cigar companies are ecstatic, and so is Fidel Castro.

A *Washington Post* report says that in midtown Manhattan at the cocktail hour, every plush seat in Club Macanudo is taken, and the air is so thick you could probably smoke a whole pig right on the bar and no one would notice. I would, I love bacon.

Omigod! What have we wrought!

Cigar magazines are springing up like crabgrass across the trotted plain.

The number of cigars brought in to the United States has risen threefold. From 1993 to 1995, cigar consumption rose 3.42 billion to 3.97 billion, and in 1996, cigar association estimates show that consumption reached 4.4 billion

Once I tasted a cigar, well, that is my boyfriend lit one for me, and told me to inhale. The smoke caught in my throat, choked me and I turned green, which is not my favorite color. I'm better in yellow.

Now let's see, what would a psychiatrist tell us about this new fad for women? That it is young people wanting to be cool, hip, professional, powerful and peer-happy? Or that it is a passing fancy and it just goes along with words they use, like "DOS, interface, megabytes and clueless?" The cigars seem to go with their good wine and lots of eye makeup.

The bad news is from the American Lung Association and the American Cancer Society — cigar smoking is as deadly as cigarette smoking. From the ALA: cancer deaths in men who smoke cigars are 34 percent higher than those among nonsmokers. There is a high rate of chronic pulmonary disease and laryngeal, oral and esophageal cancer with cigar consumption.

Come on, boys and girls, old fogies used to smoke stogies. Hey, bring back the hoop skirt, the bustle or the rumble seat, but for heaven's sake, and it may be heaven you're looking at, quit the cigar smoking.

Dinner for One

Have you tried it? It's not easy to do. I'm in my best short, black dress with dark stockings. I have my fake Gucci handbag and expensive earrings. I think I look cool, you know, as in sophisticated. I have on heels. This always helps to give me a feeling that the Power Rangers will win. Oh, yes, I am tall, too.

I enter the restaurant. A man at the front desk or podium — whatever they call those things that make it look like a place better than fast food — asks me while looking at my pocketbook, "Will that be two, Madame?"

And I answer, "No, just one, please."

I'm at a downtown hotel, where I am going to an important meeting. I need lunch; no martini lunch, just a yuppie salad, you know that kind with the long and stringy lettuce and roasted artichokes. And that darn little dish with olive oil in which you are meant to dab the wholesome bread. No butter allowed here in the land of the young and the restless.

So I get a table facing the ugliest mural of a cactus I've ever seen. But it's hard to get a table for one or even a table for two where ONE person can dine. Have you tried?

Traveling businessmen have been doing it for years. Doing what? Asking for a table for one, that's right just for one, OK? They tell me they still get a cold shoulder, especially if the maitre d' is in uniform with his name emblazoned on a gold label.

I have found out that many lone diners find it difficult to get a table for one.

I was talking to a scientist who travels, and I asked him how it is for a man alone when he enters a dining room.

He agreed: "When I travel, I sometimes have to wait while seven people get a table with no trouble. Even in airport dining rooms and hotel dining rooms. ... when I approach, I feel the head waiter or maitre d' bristles."

I know the feeling, for the waiters look at me as if I were carrying a dead fish in a box lunch. I feel they are thinking, "Poor thing, no friends, no lovers, no husband, no fun."

But my scientist friend says it is the same for a guy. They don't want you as they see you — smaller meal, smaller tip — and you are usually placed by the kitchen door. They don't want you taking up a cozy table for two.

Sometimes as a woman living alone, I eat out by myself. I get tired of my own cooking, veggie in a pouch or a TV dinner. And sometimes eating out makes me envious, you know, seeing other people laughing, talking and I am trying to figure out where to look while I read the pretentious menu for the fourth time. Some single diners doodle on the napkin. I find myself looking around, and that makes me look more pathetic than ever.

After I am seated, a waitress comes up to my table, and says, "Hello, my name is Pammy, and I will be your server." Ever notice that they are all named Jenny, Pammy, Taylor and Susie? They are good names, friendly names, brought on by the generation who started the cute and perky waitress trend. Tell me, have you ever heard of a ponytailed waitress with a name like Harriet or Thelma? No. But Pammy doesn't mind that I am alone because she is going to talk to me about her SAT scores.

For women over 40, the best thing to say is that you want a table for two, and after you have been sitting there for a while and finished your wine, tell the waiter, "Oh my, I guess my friend isn't coming, I'll order the sole."

Then the waiter will not move you. And you can laugh when you get home — full of food and thankful that you didn't choke on the arugula.

Press 8 for Options

I hate that. You know what I mean — the automated menu choices you get when you call places that don't have live voices, as in human-on-site responses to your question. It is, to me, one of the curses of the Information Age. It happens when you call movie houses, entertainment centers, your insurance companies, your utility companies and now your plumber or your dentist. And don't even try to call Social Security or the airlines unless you have an hour or two.

What I want to know is: Did someone lose a job because the company took on a robot voice called voice mail? Yes, of course, lots of switchboard operators lost their jobs. It makes me long for rotary phones.

The automated voices make you crazy if you are in a hurry. Right? In fact, all this robot voice proliferation stems from the fact that we are in a hurry, now more than ever. All of us are in a hurry, a hurry to buy a new car, a hurry to buy an insurance policy, a hurry to get a reservation. We really can't wait for anything or anybody anymore.

We hurry like the Mad Hatter in "Alice in Wonderland."

There is no time to stop and smell the roses, and so often the roses are plastic or silk.

Unless you could smell the roses on the phone, and THAT will come. Just think, you will dial a store for perfume and you will get some choices of fragrances brought to you via the phone lines. Ah, technology.

We have lost a lot of contact with the human touch when you have to "press 8" for more options, and I won't tell you which 800 numbers or Baltimore firms go up to 12 options and have too long a menu. But the live voice on the other end of the phone may be a thing of the past.

Of course, we are too impatient. We want everything now. Statistics show that we are driving faster. It is evident in road rage and parking-lot rage — where I've had fender benders twice. We want our food faster and our medicines faster. Run, Johnny, run.

So when it comes to "press 20 for further options," I hope when I have reached the peak of my endurance, I will be able to press B for "Buzz Off." That at least would make me laugh.

Epilogue

Are we there yet?

Are We There Yet?

This phrase has a ring so familiar to me that I should have written music to it. Raising four children and taking them places, anywhere, by car, by train, by plane, it was their constant ballad. It's a whining cry, one that could drive a parent right into a sacred Tibetan order.

Then along came five grandchildren, a new generation of singers. I heard the cry on trips between my house and firework displays or between Baltimore and Richmond, Va. Recently, my 3-year-old great-grandchild asked it on the way to McDonald's. We were five minutes away.

It's not a question that takes a lot of thought, like the questions that come later: "Mother, where do babies come from?" or "Do ants go to heaven when they die?"

And it's not as earthshaking as "I need to go to the potty," when you are doing 80 mph on the Tulsa Turnpike. But it's enough to wish they were all back in the womb.

Back in the 1950s, we would give them car games, soda pop and playing cards — remember, this was before the car seats in the back. They only asked the question once a day while crossing the country. That is, if they weren't practicing strangleholds on one another in the back seat.

Children are often impatient and self-centered in their perceptions from the back seat. We used to try to divert them with music, games and laughter. Their repetitive words now seem somewhat analogous to our generation.

We, ourselves, spent our youth and growing-up years governed by ambitions and desires to get something, get ahead, get there, even if we couldn't imagine where. We always thought a milestone would suffice: Life would be better after we got a new car, a new house, a new job, marriage, then a family. It seemed that there was always a place we wanted to be so we could proclaim, "We've made it!"

We are now in the "back seat" — longing, like the kids, and asking, "Are we there yet?" Some of us realize that there is no end point to our journey. Some of us may be there now and are comfortable with the end point. At 75 years old, I'm not sure I am there yet. Are you? I am not sure I've done what I wanted to do yet, even at my age.

Digging for an answer to my own question, I realized that as a society we are not there. While the haves are enjoying their new cars and technology and things of substance, the have-nots are still in the underside searching for food or housing. We have added to our possessions, but subtracted from our values. I feel that "We have miles to go before we sleep," with apologies to Robert Frost.

Newsman Tom Brokaw lauded our generation as the greatest in his book, "The Greatest Generation." Thanks, but I still think there are deep valleys of despair. We have too many guns, school violence, kids shooting kids, kids shooting up, street gangs, hatred, car chases, murder, anger and animosity. There's a kind of war going on in our country between those who perceive us as the peacekeepers abroad and those who just want peace in their own living spaces. For an industrialized nation, we seem lost between high tech and low behavior. Peace seems as illusive as ever.

Will the millennium backfire or will it help? Will we reach some kind of truce with what we have wrought? We may be having some sort of a millennium celebration that we may not deserve. We have conquered outer space, but not our inner space — the spirit and the soul. In Thomas Moore's bestseller, "Care of the Soul," he writes: "The great malady of the 20th century implicated in all of our troubles and affecting us individually and socially, is the loss of soul..." Perhaps we need to reclaim our accumulative souls to be there. Heaven seems farther away than yesteryear's version. And the ties that bind need to be laced with love and levity. Like children in the back seat, we should lighten up with laughter and, hey, listen to the music of the day.

Acknowledgements

These columns could not have been written without my husband, Guy, whose love, support and optimism were always with me. Fifty-four years of marriage was a lifetime of laughter, tears and hope.

I also want to thank my four children, now grown people and on their own, thank goodness! They were, and are, supportive of my job and gave me the ideas and inspiration to write a general commentary column: Sally Chisolm Buck, Guy M. Chisolm, Susie Chisolm Struever and Richard Chisolm. Also, thanks to their spouses, Lyle Buck, Laura Chisolm, Fred Struever and Meg Chisolm.

Thanks to my five grandchildren for their contributions to my columns and to the four great-grandchildren who make me smile and feel good that I lived this long.

Special thanks to my fine and patient editors at the Baltimore *Evening Sun*: the late Philip Heisler, who hired me, and the ones who stood by me — Miles, Ed, Mike, Ernie, Ray and others — you know who you are.

To the staff at *The Baltimore Sun* Library, especially Dee, thanks.

A very special thanks to Melinda Greenberg, my editor at *Fifty-Plus* and the editor of this book, who worked tirelessly on the project.

And before I close, I want to say thanks to my very close friends who always encouraged me and suggested topics for my columns: Jeanne and Bob Kendig, Catherine Zelsman, Ruth Hehl, Freeman Baldridge, Ellen London, Mary Beth Molony, Josephine Atwater, Julie and Homer Schamp and Nancy Townsend and her husband, David Townsend, who happens to be my favorite and only brother and who knows when to laugh.

About the author

Elise Chisolm was a member of the Baltimore *Evening Sun's* staff for 26 years. Her work has been published in four national magazines and her column was carried over the *Los Angeles Times-Washington Post* News Service to many cities and Canada. She retired from the *Sun* in January 1990. Since then, she has written a monthly column, "That's Life," for *Fifty-Plus Magazine*. Ms. Chisolm also teaches creative writing at the Catonsville Senior Center. The mother of four grown children, she has five grandchildren and four great-grandchildren. Ms. Chisolm credits her family with inspiring many of her columns. She lives in Mount Washington.